REMEMBERING GOD'S MERCY

Kevin O'Gorman SMA

Remembering God's
MERCY

Luke's Virtue of Compassion

ST PAULS

© 2015 ST PAULS Publishing
Moyglare Road
Maynooth
Co. Kildare
Ireland

Published by: ST PAULS Publishing

ISBN: 978-1-911178-00-2

Set by ST PAULS

Cover: Middledot

Printed by Melita Press, Malta

ST PAULS is an activity of the priests and brothers of the Society of St Paul who proclaim the Gospel through the media of social communication.

Introduction

At the conclusion of her account of *Luke, His Audience and Purpose* scripture scholar Barbara Reid makes the following observation: 'It has long been observed that Luke may consistently bring up a particular topic, but he does not speak about it consistently'.[1] In support of this traditional thesis she quotes G.W.H. Lampe's description of the evangelist's style as holding 'a large number of threads in his hand at once, introducing first one and then another into a somewhat untidy and ill-defined pattern, without allowing any one of them to predominate over the rest as to give unity and coherence to the whole'.[2] Reid's reference to the consistency of Luke in his return to a particular theme throughout his Gospel may ultimately be something that can only be settled by biblical scholars and theologians. The substitution of 'thread' for 'topic' may be symbolic for understanding Luke's style and the subjects he treats. I propose to follow the thread of 'mercy' throughout this Gospel. Whether this turns out to be a 'golden thread' in the text and theology of the most artistic of the evangelists is a judgement call to be made after consideration of the numerous references to 'mercy' in the

---

[1]   *Choosing the Better Part? – Women in the Gospel of Luke* (Collegeville, MN: The Liturgical Press, 1996), 20

[2]   Ibid

overall text of Luke. I take support from the statement of John F. O' Grady that 'often enough scholars and readers will characterize this gospel as the gospel of mercy, and rightly so'.[3]

Noting that he is 'the evangelist who makes the role of *mimesis*, imitation, most explicit', Richard A. Burridge states that 'in fact the whole of Luke-Acts is full of examples to follow or to avoid for moral conduct'.[4] An important feature of this imitation in the Gospel of Luke is its indication of the link between morality and spirituality. At the conclusion of what is probably its most well-known piece, the parable of the Good Samaritan, Luke concludes the question to Jesus about the identity of the neighbour: '"The one who showed him mercy". Jesus said, "Go and do likewise"' (10:37). Imitation by showing and doing the mercy of God is a leitmotif that links many of the stories, scenes and sayings of Jesus in Luke. (Throughout Luke refers to the evangelist, *Luke* in his gospel.)

This work has been in gestation for a number of years and has been given fresh impetus by Pope Francis' insistence on proclaiming and practising mercy as the mission of the Church. Hopefully it can contribute something to the convergence of *Luke* in the (Sunday) Lectionary and *Mercy* in the mission of the Church for the coming year (and beyond). I have written it as a moral theologian and preface it with the spirit of the

---

[3] *The Four Gospels and the Jesus Tradition* (New York: Paulist Press, 1989), 226

[4] *Imitating Jesus – An Inclusive Approach to New Testament Ethics* (Cambridge, U.K.: Eerdmans, 2007), 280

following statement: 'This is not a form-critical or closely argued philological commentary for the professional biblical scholar. I seek here to represent Luke's gospel as, by faithful men and women for more than nineteen centuries, it has been normatively read – namely, as a faithful report of the life, ministry, and person of Jesus the Christ – and to do so with an eye to providing insights from those who would read it in "the company of the saints and faithful of all ages".[5] I wish to thank Bernard Treacy OP, editor of *Doctrine and Life* for permission to reproduce Chapter One and the Scholastic Trust of the College for its support.

Kevin O'Gorman SMA
Saint Patrick's College
Maynooth

---

[5] David Lyle Jeffrey (Author's Preface), *Luke* (Grand Rapids, Michigan: Brazos Press, 2012), xv

Contents

Introduction

Chapter 1   Bible, Believing and Being Moral 11

Chapter 2   Looking at Luke 32

Chapter 3   Mercy From On High 53

Chapter 4   Miracles of Mercy 68

Chapter 5   Parables of Pity 81

Chapter 6   Luke's Model of Mercy 119

Chapter 7   Making a Virtue of Mercy 147

Postscript   Looking at Mercy and Luke through a
            Papal Lens 163

Select Bibliography 173

Chapter One

Bible, Believing and Being Moral

'Special care is to be taken for the improvement of moral theology. Its scientific presentation, drawing more fully on the teaching of holy scripture, should highlight the lofty vocation of the Christian faithful and their obligation to bring forth fruit in charity for the life of the world'.[6]

'Special care...'

The statement by the Second Vatican Council that the science of moral theology needed special attention was hardly surprising. While its subject matter – the Christian moral life – stands in perpetual need of 'improvement' through the ongoing conversion of individuals and communities that constitute the Church, moral theology was the latest branch of theology to begin a process of renewal in the decade prior to the calling of the Council. The so-called manual tradition had dominated moral theology for centuries since the Council of Trent. The subject had settled into a staid system and stood in need of a major shake-up. Designed to serve as textbooks for seminarians

---

[6] *Optatam Totius, Decree on the Training of Priests*, 16, in ed Austin Flannery *Vatican Council II – The Basic Sixteen Documents* (Dublin: Dominican Publications, 2007)

to prepare them for the sacrament of penance their authors could have profitably and prophetically taken the advice that J.K. Galbraith once offered economists (substituting the word *moral* for *economic*): 'The problem with most economic theories is not original error but uncorrected obsolescence'.[7] I have elsewhere described the difficulties with the approach to and analysis of morality adopted in these texts as *Arteriosclerosis in Manualibus,*[8] a hardening of the moral-theological arteries which narrowed the focus of morality to acts and reduced the role of faith to providing the proverbial layer of theological icing (and a thin one at that) for the moral cake, the basic contents of which were sourced almost singularly from within the natural law tradition.

In particular the method of using and understanding sacred scripture in moral theology was seriously problematic. This resembled a 'cut and paste approach' which saw the selection of sayings and sentences from the Bible chosen to confirm conclusions which had been arrived at through the use of reason. In real terms the text and theology of the Bible was superfluous to the vision of morality envisaged by and expressed in the manuals. Given the encouragement for the rooting of theology in scripture and the exhortation to engage in critical biblical studies which were expressed by different

---

[7]   Quoted in Raphael Gallagher, 'The Manual System of Moral Theology Since the Death of Alphonsus', *Irish Theological Quarterly* 51 (1985) : 1-16, here 9

[8]   'From Principles to Disciples: The Moral Theology of Timothy E. O'Connell', in *Faithful Witness – Glimpses of the Kingdom*, eds. Joe Egan & Brendan McConvery (Dublin: Milltown Institute, 2005), 213-225, here 214

popes long before the beginning of the Council, its statement that the scientific character of moral theology should be connected with the Bible is consistent with the concomitant call that 'all the preaching of the Church, as indeed the entire Christian religion, should be nourished and ruled by sacred Scripture'.[9]

'draw more fully on the teaching of holy Scripture'

In the two decades after Vatican II moral theology devoted a lot of energy to examining how and to what extent the discipline could draw upon the teaching of the Bible. This exploration developed into an exchange of opinions between two schools of thought which became known as the 'autonomy' and 'faith-ethic' positions. These two approaches to the analysis and application of sacred scripture in the undertaking of 'Christian morality' advanced from diverse angles and arrived at different answers. The 'autonomists' asserted that there was one morality, applicable to both believer and non-believer alike and thus in terms of content 'Christian morality' could not be materially contrasted with human morality. Following the natural law tradition of Catholic moral theology the advocates of autonomy argued that the communication of the moral law in the order of creation meant that there was a universal basis which underpinned a common morality for both Christians and non-Christians. Asserting that the role of

---

[9]   *Dei Verbum, Dogmatic Constitution on Divine Revelation* , 2, in *Vatican Council II – The Basic Sixteen Documents*

faith and revelation in relation to the moral life of believers is concerned with context and not content, motivation and ultimate meaning rather than manifesting moral norms, the 'autonomy' school denied that scripture supplied 'surplus' moral norms which separated believers from their brothers and sisters in the world. The Bible offered encouragement for and examples of moral living and 'the teaching of holy scripture' transmitted generic and not specific moral truths for the Christian faithful.

Not surprisingly, as the name suggests, the 'faith-ethic' approach disagreed with this overview of moral obligation outside of the content of the Bible and Church teaching. Rejecting the reductionism of relying on the natural law and reason theologians of this school claimed that, because human nature is fallen, it cannot supply the fullness of Christian morality. Moreover, they maintained that the role of faith in the moral life of Christians and the Church could not be relegated to the spectrum of interior states which the 'autonomy' school had articulated in terms of vision, horizon, stance, motivation and intentionality. Thus William E. May asserted that 'Christian faith can give rise to specific norms proper to the Christian way of life' and that 'faith generates specific norms which could not be known without it'.[10] John R. Donahue described the debate – and disagreement – about the role of scripture as a source of such norms in succinct terms: 'The fundamental question is whether the Bible provides any distinctive moral teaching

---

[10] *An Introduction to Moral Theology* (Indiana: Our Sunday Visitor, 1991), 192

that is not accessible, at least in principle, to human reason (as affirmed by the moral autonomy school) or whether biblical revelation gives a new *content* to morality (the position of the *Glaubensethik* [ethics of belief or faith] school'.[11] A major line of analysis of the debate devolved to discussion of the terms 'specificity' and 'distinctiveness' as these applied to the moral life of Christians. In relation to the role of the Bible and its interpretation advocates of a *specific* demand of Christian morality argued for a 'revealed morality' while proponents of a *distinctive* dimension in the moral life of Christians argued for a 'revealed reality', to employ terms used by Richard M. Gula.[12]

The idea of drawing from scripture immediately suggests the biblical image of the well. Isaiah exuberantly expresses the joy of 'draw[ing] water from the wells of salvation' (12:3) while John elucidates Jesus' encounter with the 'Samaritan woman who came to draw water' as the exchange which effects conversion not only for her but also through her for many in the community. In its document on 'New Age' the Pontifical Councils for Culture and Interreligious Dialogue declare that 'the fact that the story takes place by a well is significant [as] Jesus offers the woman "a spring...welling up to eternal life" [Jn 4:14] '.[13] The image of the well both indicates water as

---

[11] 'The Challenge of the Biblical Renewal to Moral Theology', in *Riding Time Like A River – The Catholic Moral Tradition Since Vatican II*, ed. William J. O'Brien (Washington, DC:Georgetown University Press, 1993), 59-80, here 62

[12] See his *Reason Informed By Faith* (New York: Paulist Press, 1989), Chapter 12

[13] *Jesus Christ, the Bearer of the Water of Life: A Christian Reflection on the New Age*, *Origins*, 32 (13 February 2003), 569-592, here 585

the symbol of purification and salvation alongside the hidden depths of its source. Inviting those who are interested to look beneath the surface the well that is the Word of God intimates the interior dimension of morality. While not ignoring the importance of acts, the 'flow' of the moral life seeks to see them as the incarnation of inner dispositions and integrate them into the life of virtue. For Christians the image of the well is an invitation to continually plumb the depths where God's grace and human freedom dovetail.

However, moral theology has moved on from the manual system with its simplistic approach to scripture as a source of texts for teaching. The theological task of drawing from the moral teaching of the Bible calls for rigorous research and reflection on several counts. The Pontifical Biblical Commission admits that there is a copious and complex combination of moral categories, codes and concepts contained in its corpus and that 'the Bible reflects a considerable moral development, which finds its completion in the New Testament'.[14] Moreover, the Commission acknowledges that the hermeneutical task involved is intricate as 'the New Testament itself is not easy to interpret in the area of morality, for it often makes use of imagery, frequently in a way that is paradoxical or even provocative'.[15] Examples of the former approach are found in Luke's formulation of the Beatitudes, such as 'Blessed are you who are hungry now, for you will be filled/blessed are you who

[14] *The Interpretation of the Bible in the Church* (Vatican City: Libreria Editrice Vaticana,1993), 109
[15] Ibid, 110

weep now, for you will laugh' (6:21), and of the latter attitude in his invocation of the saying of Jesus: 'Whoever is not with me is against me, and whoever does not gather with me scatters' (11:23). Nevertheless, the Commission expresses confidence that moral theologians can draw from the wealth of scriptural teaching even on questions where 'the response may be that no biblical text explicitly addresses the problem proposed [since] the witness of the Bible, taken within the framework of the forceful dynamic that governs it as a whole, will certainly indicate a fruitful direction to follow.'[16]

'throw light upon the exalted vocation of the faithful in Christ'

Vatican II espouses a vision of all the Christian faithful in their pilgrim journey towards the Kingdom as the People of God. This vision involves an invitation to all the faithful to support in the earthly mission of the Church and share in its eschatological destiny. The identity of the 'faithful' as the common classification of belonging to the Church is indicated by the *Code of Canon Law* (which is itself inspired by the texts of the Council): 'Christ's faithful are those who, since they are incorporated into Christ through Baptism, are constituted the people of God... They are called...to exercise the mission which God entrusted to the Church to fulfil in the world.'[17] This 'exalted vocation' is expressed in Vatican II by the 'universal call to holiness' which extends to the whole People of God:

---

[16]   Ibid
[17]   *The Code of Canon Law* (London: Colins, 1983), c 204.1

'Therefore, all in the Church...are called to holiness...This holiness of the Church is shown constantly in the faithful and so it must be; it is expressed in many ways by the individuals who, each in their own state of life, tend to the perfection of charity'.[18] This call to perfection stands in marked contrast to the minimalism of the manuals of moral theology prior to the Council which considered the Christian life negatively. One has only to compare the position of Thomas Slater – 'They are not intended for edification, nor do they hold up a high ideal of Christian perfection for the imitation of the faithful'[19] – with the proclamation of the Council – 'The Lord Jesus, divine teacher and model of all perfection, preached holiness of life, which he both initiates and brings to perfection, to each and every one of his disciples no matter what their condition of life: "You, therefore, must be perfect, as your heavenly Father is perfect" (Mt 5:4-8)'.[20] (This emphasis on perfection resonates with the Latin – *Theologia moralis perficiendae* – perfecting moral theology – in the original conciliar text.)

Replete with references to perfection – 'tend to the perfection of charity', 'perfect in their lives that holiness which they have received from God', 'reach this perfection' – these paragraphs promoting the common call to holiness provide the true goal for the Christian faithful to aspire to and articulate the agenda for an authentic renewal of

---

[18] *Lumen Gentium, Dogmatic Constitution on the Church, 39, in Vatican Council II – The Basic Sixteen Documents*

[19] *A Manual of Moral Theology* (New York: Benziger, 1908), 6

[20] *Lumen Gentium, Dogmatic Constitution on the Church, 40, in Vatican Council II – The Basic Sixteen Documents*

moral theology. Furthermore, holiness and human life are inextricably connected in the claim that 'it is therefore quite clear that all Christians in whatever state or walk in life are called 'to the fullness of Christian life and to the perfection of charity, this holiness is conducive to a more human way of living even in society here on earth'.[21] Thus the call to holiness does not draw the Christian faithful away from the world but drives them to engage with the world to develop a better way of being and acting in it. Moral theology contributes to the discernment of this way by reflecting on how divine grace and human freedom dovetail in history.

'their obligation to bring forth fruit'

Reference to the 'obligation' of the Christian faithful jars somewhat with the previous mention of their 'exalted vocation'. This contrast of terminology corresponds to the variety of theological models in viewing morality as call or commandment. In the wake of Vatican II the renewed 'scientific presentation' of moral theology opted more for an invitation-response schema rather than an order-obligation structure. This shift of stance to a more personalist and relational perspective rather than a positivist and rule programme is reflected in the change in the title given by the renowned Redemptorist moral theologian Bernard Häring to his major works, from *The Law of Christ* in the *1950s to Free and Faithful in Christ* more than twenty years later. Indeed it has been suggested that this latter title could be complemented and completed by the alliterative addition

---

21   Ibid

of fruitful, to furnish its biblical foundation and focus, viz. *Free, Faithful and Fruitful in Christ.*

The image of bearing fruit has a strong biblical basis. Luke presents the ministry of John in terms of producing fruit 'in keeping with repentance... Yes, even now the axe is being laid to the root of the trees, so that any tree failing to produce good fruit will be cut down and thrown on the fire' (3:8-9). This expression of repentance and the response it requires is expounded later by Jesus when he exclaims that 'every tree can be told by its own fruit' (6:44). With the equation of 'sound fruit' and 'store of goodness in their hearts'/ 'rotten fruit' and 'store of badness' (6:45), the evangelist emphasizes the evidence of conversion as exemplifying what Jesus called for from his disciples. Coming towards the end of Jesus' 'Sermon on the Plain,' this is more than a metaphor for morality. In keeping with the Baptist's reference to repentance, bearing good fruit illustrates the integrity and identity of those who respond to the Gospel invitation of Jesus.

In his proclamation of the Reign of God Jesus often drew his teaching from the natural world. Using images of seed(s) growing and dying and speaking about gathering or scattering Jesus nurtured – and on occasion needled – his hearers to recognize God's initiative and respond to it. By contrasting the delight of harvesting with the danger of hoarding Jesus was able to balance celebration and condemnation. The parable of the sower is common to the Synoptics. While interpretations of the identity of the 'sower' include both Jesus himself and early Christian missionaries, Luke's interest is in identifying the seed as 'the word of God' (8:11). In his interpretation he shifts from naturalistic imagery to human intentionality, highlighting 'the ones who, when they hear the word, hold it fast in an honest and good heart, and bear fruit with patient endurance' (8:15). In contrast there are others who, like the 'wicked tenants' in the parable of the same name, reject the right of the householder 'to get his share of the produce of the vineyard from them' (Lk 20:10). The expectation of earning a return from the vineyard is frustrated again and again until, finally, the owner's son and heir is sent and suffers execution. While interpretations of this parable include the engagement of Jesus with the Temple establishment and the experience of the early church, in ethical terms it is about accountability and the ensuing judgement that arises. As Klyne R. Snodgrass comments: 'Like so many others, the parable is primarily about response. Will people respond to the claims God has on their lives or reject His messengers in favour of their own agenda? Will they live productively to "produce fruits" for God?'[22]

As Bernard Häring notes, 'the Gospel of John, Chapter 15, uses the symbol of fruitfulness repeatedly'.[23] Moving from the natural to the interpersonal, the metaphor indicates the intimacy and interaction between Jesus and those who hear and heed his word: 'I am the vine, you are the branches. Just as the branch cannot bear fruit by itself unless it abides in the vine, neither can you unless you abide in me' (Jn 15:5). Identifying Jesus' relation as rooted in the Father who is 'the vinegrower', John interprets 'the vine and branches' as an invitation to communion in which

---

[22] *Stories with Intent – A Comprehensive Guide to the Parables of Jesus*, (Cambridge, U.K.: Eerdmans, 2008), 297

[23] *Free and Faithful in Christ*, vol. 2, (Middlegreen, Slough; St Pauls, 1979), 27

fruitfulness flourishes. The 'branches' are identified as being the 'disciples' of Jesus by virtue of being in him and bearing 'much fruit' (15:8). This fruitfulness is a harvest which heaps glory on God the Father. However, this requires a response to divine grace rooted in human freedom, as Xavier Léon-Dufour states: 'The disciple, who has become, thanks to the Word, a branch of the only true vine, remains a branch only by personal faithfulness, continually renewed. Personal consent is always required. Thus, while a beneficiary of the action of the Shepherd, the disciple participates in the action of the vine: the disciple who remains grafted onto the vine is the co-author of the fruit that the vine bears. The goal of grafting (15:2) is precisely to maintain a perfect "synergy" between the Son and his disciples'.[24] The conjoining of the branches to the vine is a metaphor of both moral conformity to and spiritual communion with Jesus. Thus the evangelist emphasizes that the moral life of Christians is not extrinsic but emerges from their inner belonging to the Father and Son. The organic outcome of being in Christ is bearing fruit. Inhering in the grace of God is the 'indicative' which grounds the 'imperative' of being good and bearing fruit.[25]

The contrast between bearing good and bad fruit (or no fruit) originates in the teaching of Jesus and finds a theological outlet in the texts of the Gospels. Paul gives this image of fruitful-less/ness classic expression in his *Letter to the Galatians*. Opposing

---

[24]   *To Act According to the Gospel*, (Peabody, Mass: Hendrickson, 2005), 102

[25]   The logic of the indicative and the imperative is a distinguishing mark not only of Paul's ethics but of biblical ethics in general. Throughout the Bible human behaviour is always considered in the context of the underlying and overarching relationship with God'. Brian Rosner, 'Paul's ethics', in *The Cambridge Companion to St Paul*, ed. James G. Dunn, (Cambridge: Cambridge University Press,), 212-223, here 222

the experience of licentiousness with that of liberty he elucidates their respective effects. With two lists – of vices and virtues respectively – Paul characterizes the 'works of the flesh' (5:19) and the 'fruit of the Spirit' (5:22). The latter are so labelled as, according to Daniel Harrington and James Keenan, 'a way of acknowledging their origin and dynamism with the Holy Spirit [and] are ways by which the Holy Spirit dwelling within the Christian empowers good and helpful actions'.[26] Bearing such fruit(s) is witness to the presence and power of the Holy Spirit at work in those who believe in God and belong to Christ. The list of fruit(s) looks to the inner dispositions and the deeds they generate against which 'there is no law' (5:23). As John links the fruitfulness of the disciples to being rooted in the love of God which Jesus reveals and represents Paul lists 'love' as first in 'the fruit of the Spirit'.

'in charity for the life of the world'

James G. Dunn describes the 'love command' as the agreed fundamental principle in Christian ethics [which] serves to tie together the major themes of New Testament theology: God as characterized by steadfast love and mercy – "God is love" (1Jn 4:8...and Jesus' commanding his followers to love their neighbour as themselves (Mk 12:29-31). *'Ubi caritas, deus ibi est.'*[27] Developing the vine/branch(es) relationship John integrates the identity of the disciples as friends of Jesus with their bearing the fruit of love. Paul's 'Hymn to Love' in 1 Corinthians holds love as the highest value, highlighting simply

---

26   *Paul and Virtue Ethics* (New York: Rowan & Littlefield, 2010), 111
27   *New Testament Theology – An Introduction* (Nashville: Abingdon Press, 2009), 151

that 'Love never ends' (13:8). This is not a simplistic statement of love as the list of qualities show. The love that Christians are called to live is rooted in and received from God, charity as 'the theological virtue of love, *agape* in us.'[28] However, while the command to love is, in Dunn's words, 'that most fundamental of insights'[29], the task remains to interpret this 'insight' in realistic and responsible ways. Moral theologians and Christian ethicists want to avoid Paul Ramsey's rejoinder to Joseph Fletcher that love runs through his *Situation Ethics* 'like a greased pig'!

David M. McCarthy lists the task(s) of moral theology in the following terms: 'Moral theology, in large part, is our attempt to understand what we are saying about human life and God's love for the world through what we ought to do, through our articulation of what is good and the kinds of actions, institutions, and practices that sustain what is good'.[30] Looking at the link between 'human life and God's love for the world' is the lens that moral theology uses in interpreting its scientific status. The intersection of human life in all its demands – from sexual through social to spiritual – with divine love in all its dimensions – 'the breadth and length and height and depth [of] the love of Christ' (Eph 3:18-19) – informs the interests and inspires the inquiries of moral theologians. Working 'in the light of the Gospel and

---

[28] James P. Hanigan, *As I Have Loved You – The Challenge of Christian Ethics* (New York: Paulist Press, 1986), 153

[29] Ibid. For a detailed treatment of 'love' in moral theology see Edward Collins Vacek, *Love, Human and Divine – The Heart of Christian Ethics* (Washington, DC: Georgetown University Press, 1994)

[30] 'Love in Fundamental Moral Theology' in ed James Keating, *Moral Theology: New Directions and Fundamental Issues* (New York: Paulist Press, 2004), 181-206, here 182-183

of human experience'[31], they attempt to analyse and articulate the incarnational implications of Christian faith. To paraphrase (partly) Saint Anselm's classic definition of theology, moral theology is faith seeking understanding in love and undertaking in hope. The relevance of a renewed moral theology was reflected by the fact that 'the few moral theologians at the Council were eventually enlisted into the preparation of the Constitution on the Church in the *Modern World'*.[32] The author's emphasis on the *Modern World* highlights the historical awareness which alongside, a more positive attitude to earthly realities, has been a hallmark of moral theology since the Council.

The Council's call to a renewed moral theology to be concerned with the world commits believers, both personally and communally, to a responsibility for the good of all people. This responsibility requires an ongoing dialogue with non-Christians and non-believers about the discernment of this (common) good and the development of 'the kinds of actions, institutions, and practices' that support, strengthen and, if necessary, suffer for this good. Specifically, moral theology seeks to defend the dignity of human life, develop strategies for its flourishing and deepen the sense of its final destiny. Thus responsibility for the world reflects the conviction and concern that, in the words of Pope Benedict XVI, 'for the Church, charity is not a kind of welfare activity which could equally well be left to others,

---

[31]   *Gaudium et Spes, Pastoral Constitution on the Church in the Modern World*, 46, in *Vatican Council II – The Basic Sixteen Documents*

[32]   Damien Heath, 'Special Attention Needs to be given to the Development of Moral Theology – *Optatam Totius* n 16', *The Australasian Catholic Record*, 63(1986):302-312, here 303

but is a part of her nature, an indispensable expression of her very being'.[33] Bearing 'fruit in charity for the life of the world' is not an optional extra but a fundamental obligation for the community of the Christian faithful. Pope Francis underscores this in *The Joy of the Gospel,* particularly in Chapter Four, 'The Social Dimension of Evangelization'. While the call of the Council for the renewal of moral theology is contained in the *Decree on the Training of Priests* it is not confined to the seminary audience(s) that the manuals addressed. A year after its publication Josef Neuner stated that 'it speaks of the necessity of basing moral theology more on Scripture and of deriving the demands of morality from the sublimity of the Christian vocation and Christian responsibility for the world'.[34] The combination of sublimity and responsibility here highlights the hinge between holiness and humanity in history.

From Teachings to Teacher

Vatican II's lines about moral theology sounded the death knell for the manuals of moral theology, which had admittedly been in the throes for some time anyway. Their focus on the law and the sinful side of human activity favoured a minimalism as found in the quote from Slater above. Responding to the call of the Council moral theology could be said to have intensified, if not initiated its own course of conversion. This ongoing process has involved moral theologians in dialogue – and sometimes

---

[33] *Deus caritas est, God is Love,* (Vatican City: Libreria Editrice Vaticana, 2006), 25

[34] *Commentary on the Documents of Vatican II,* Vol 2(II), ed Herbert Vorgrimler (London: Burns & Oates, 1969), 399

disagreement – among themselves and with others, scripture scholars obviously but also systematic theologians and those working in the field of spirituality. Two outcomes of this dialogue are worth highlighting, the recovery of virtue and the relationship between morality and spirituality. In parallel with its partner in philosophical ethics Charles E. Curran and Lisa A. Fullam state that 'virtue is a most important subject in moral theology [while] until a few decades ago it lived mostly in the shadows of the discipline'.[35] Recovering the roots of the theological virtues in the Bible moral theologians seek to relate these to the cardinal or moral virtues. The status of discipleship has become central to the consideration of moral theology as reflection on the Christian moral life and this is seen in the renewed emphasis on the part that both morality and spirituality play together. Curran and Fullam identify 'the beginning of the shift in moral theology from a rule-based system to a more holistic model of Christian discipleship arose with the turn to scripture and ascetical theology in the mid-twentieth century'.[36] Josef Fuchs once stated (in a seminar) that the two most important words in Christian tradition come from the Council of Chalcedon, those concerning the two natures of Christ, 'distinct, not separate'. With its roots in the Bible moral theology recognizes that in the context of discipleship it is possible to distinguish between but not separate the spiritual from what is moral. Fifty years after the

---

[35] *Foreword*, in *Virtue – Readings in Moral Theology No. 16*, eds Charles E. Curran and Lisa A. Fullam, (New York; Paulist Press, 2011), ix

[36] *Foreword*, in *Ethics and Spirituality – Readings in Moral Theology No. 17*, eds Charles E. Curran and Lisa A. Fullam (New York: Paulist Press, 2014), vii

promulgation of the *Decree* with its 'two-sentence statement on moral theology' the discipline can be said to have taken it on board, that is, 'to incorporate the scriptures in [the] study of moral theology and to embrace more clearly the virtue of charity and the role of discipleship'.[37]

Christina A. Astorga states the necessity for a nexus between the Bible and moral theology:

> If moral theology is to be a genuine theological discipline, it must be rooted in scripture. Scripture ought to inform and shape moral theology as a field of study. The place of scripture in moral theology is necessary and essential, but the question of how it is to be realized and by which method opens a whole new discussion with which both Catholic and Protestant moral theologians continue to engage.[38]

Astorga articulates two uses of scripture in moral theology, 'illuminative or prescriptive'.[39] The 'illuminative' inspires an overall vision of the moral life and is imagined as a story, interpreted by narrative criticism. The 'prescriptive' posits scripture as a source of information and is imagined as a set of texts, interpreted primarily by historical criticism. These two models of the relationship between scripture and moral theology could be correlated with what Richard M. Gula called 'Revealed

---

[37] James F. Keenan, *A History of Catholic Moral Theology in the Twentieth Century – From Confessing Sins to Liberating Consciousness*, (New York: Continuum, 2010), 95

[38] *Catholic Moral Theology & Social Ethics* (Maryknoll, New York: Orbis Books, 2014), 107

[39] Ibid

Reality' and 'Revealed Morality' respectively.[40] However, the use of scripture in moral theology needs a method that transcends the narrative and normative. This third option offers a different optic, the transformative, which puts the focus not on the process of using the Bible in moral theology or its product but rather on the persons undertaking it. Imagined in terms of invitation and response this third model could be called 'Revealed Relationality'. Rooted in Jesus' inauguration of the Reign of God, his invitation, 'Follow me', indicates that a morality rooted in a personal response rather than a record or rules is congruent with this call. The call to repent and receive the Good News of God's Reign is the response that results in what Paul J. Wadell refers to as 'a transformed and transforming way of life'.[41] This model of 'Revealed Relationality' is well reflected in the Pontifical Biblical Commission document *The Bible and Morality*:

> Jesus proclaims the nearness of the kingdom of God, to be heard and accepted through conversion and faith. A change of mentality is needed, new ways of thought and a new vision, conditioned by God's kingdom, perceived through the wisdom of faith. The principal purpose of Jesus' mission is to reveal God, the Father (Mt 11:27), and his reign, his way of acting. This revelation occurs throughout the whole of Jesus' mission, by his preaching, his mighty works, his passion and his resurrection.[42]

---

[40]   *Reason Informed By Faith - Foundations of Catholic Morality* (New York: Paulist Press, 1989), 172-182

[41]   'Christology and the Christian Life', *Journal of Moral Theology*, 2(2013), 1-23, here 11

[42]   (Vatican City: Libreria Editrice Vaticana, 2008), 45

By focussing on Jesus' mission to reveal the Reign of God in its totality and not reducing it to a set of teachings, moral theology is able to articulate the achievement of 'drawing more fully' from scripture. By abandoning the proof text approach of the manuals and allying itself with the results of biblical research moral theology has been able to advance its own scientific status as the theological space where ethics and Christology are entwined with ecclesiology and eschatology. The transformative agenda of moral theology is rooted in responsibility for the world and its relation to the Reign of God. Recognizing the need to return continually to the well that is God's word moral theology can find there a reservoir for its own ongoing renewal as well as recommending conversion as the cornerstone of the Christian moral life. To change the metaphor, scripture is the school of God's word in which moral theology is, to use a phrase of its patron Saint Alphonsus, 'always reading and learning something new'.[43] By its attention to the school of God's word in which Christ is the teacher and the Holy Spirit tutor the moral theologians can aim to be like Matthew's 'master of a household who brings out of his treasure what is new and what is old' (13:52).

While there is no explicit reference to Christ in the two-sentence statement of the *Decree* about the need to develop the discipline moral theologians had been writing about the Christological focus of the biblical renewal that would serve as a basis for renewal. Writing a year before its promulgation

---

[43]   Quoted in Heath, 'Special Attention Needs to be given to the Development of Moral Theology – *Optatam Totius* n 16', 312

Enda McDonagh stated that 'In its growth and composition, in its gradual manifestation of God to man, in the dominant ideas which that manifestation reveals and the immediate contact with the person of Christ which it gives, the Bible must dominate the moral theologian's thinking, if he is to present Christ and his message as a way of life'.[44] Dovetailing the presentation of Christ and putting people in contact with Christ, this statement set the agenda for a moral theology devoted to developing discipleship 'as a way of life'. Writing forty years later about what the *Decree* said regarding moral theology, Gerald O'Collins expressed the fruits of 'this emphasis on a biblical teaching that feeds moral thought and practice [which] entails a Christ-centred vision of the Bible and hence the conviction that Christ should be the very soul of moral reflection and conduct'.[45] With a renewed focus on the theological virtues (and their relation to the moral virtues) moral theology is well set to present Christ and his paschal way as 'perceived through the wisdom of faith', practised by works of charity and prayed by words of hope. In biblical terms believing and being moral are brought together in the two-sentence statement about 'living a good life in Christ... [and] doing right' (1 Pet 3:16-17).[46]

---

[44] 'Moral Theology: The Need for Renewal' in *Moral Theology Renewed*, ed Enda McDonagh (Dublin: Gill and Son, 1965), 13-30, here 21

[45] *Living Vatican II – The 21st Council for the 21st Century* (New York: Paulist Press, 2006), 86

[46] From *Second Reading for Sixth Sunday of Easter, Year A, Jerusalem Bible* version

Chapter Two

Looking at Luke

'It is not surprising that virtually every sort of Jesus reconstructed by scholars in this generation is based solidly on the Jesus of the Gospel of Luke, for this is the Jesus we most admire – political, public, prophetic, the one who includes the marginal and challenges the status of the powerful.'[47]

Scripture and moral theology/Christian ethics

Since the promulgation of the Council's call for moral theology to draw 'more fully on the teachings of holy scripture' the volume of literature on the subject has been vast. As Raymond F. Collins states, 'the literature on ethics in the New Testament is quite vast'.[48] While his comment about it being 'both foolhardy and impossible' to try to summarize this is wise, it is important to suggest something of the scope and spectrum of this literature. Jesuits Daniel J. Harrington and James F. Keenan offer an inter-disciplinary approach (involving a scripture scholar and moral theologian) through the avenue of virtue ethics.[49] The subtitle

---

[47] 'Reconstructing Christ', *America*, 203(2-9 August 2010): 11-13, here 12

[48] *Christian Morality –Biblical Foundations*, (Notre Dame: University of Notre Dame Press, 1986), 41

[49] *Jesus and Virtue Ethics* (New York: Rowman & Littlefield, *Paul and Virtue Ethics*, New York: Rowman & Littlefield, 2010)

of their two books – *Building Bridges between New Testament Studies and Moral Theology* – indicates that their 'work is not a comprehensive portrait of Jesus and his teachings or a full-scale survey of New Testament moral teachings or a systematic reflection on how the Bible has been used in moral theology [but] explores some topics in the Synoptic [and Pauline] tradition to see where the encounter between biblical studies might go'.[50] Ben Witherington III's *The Indelible Image* presents 'a sampling of the *doing of theology and ethics* in the twenty-seven books in the New Testament.[51]

The *'doing of theology and ethics'* is the focus of the previously mentioned document *The Bible and Morality*. Its subtitle, *Biblical Roots and Christian Conduct*, is reflected in the setting of the Ten Commandments (Ex 20:2-17) set side by side with the Beatitudes (Mt 5:3-12). The situation of these texts at the very beginning of the document bears evidence of its purpose to present the moral 'teaching of holy Scripture' as proposed by Vatican II. Its method is set out in the *Preface*: 'It can be stated that in biblical anthropology the primary and basic factor is God's action, forestalling human behaviour: his gifts of grace, his call to communion. The normative complex is consequential; it shows the proper way to accept and live out God's gift'.[52] The consequence of grounding morality in the grace of God entails an experience that elicits a response which is not the statement of a law but a summons to a way of life.

---

[50]   *Jesus and Virtue Ethics* , xv
[51]   (Downers Grove, Illinois: IVP Academic, 2009), 16
[52]   *The Bible and Morality*, 7

This is the invitation to 'human beings to conform their thought and their actions to the divine model: "You shall be holy, for I the Lord your God am holy" (Lev 19:2); "Be perfect, therefore, as your heavenly Father is perfect" (Mt 5:48)'.[53] Calling this 'an important and very helpful text' which 'hopes that those who teach moral theology and engage in pastoral responsibility will avoid mere legalism, casuistry and fundamentalism' Kevin Seasoltz reiterates that 'rather than give clear and precise directives, the commission sought to recommend an approach to morality in a spirit derived from the Bible itself'.[54]

However, from the standpoint of a biblically based moral theology a significant weakness of the document is the way it deals with the Synoptic Gospels. *Matthew, Mark* and *Luke* are subsumed into a generic approach analysed in terms of 'the New Covenant in Jesus Christ as God's final gift and its moral implications'. While it may be unrealistic to expect such a document to deal fully with the diversity of New Testament moral teaching as a whole there is a danger, particularly with the Gospels, of conflating their theological content and its connection with morality (The *Gospel of John* is treated at length, along with the Johannine *Letters*, separately.). Notwithstanding the need to focus on the foundational ministry and message of Jesus there is a need to acknowledge the nuanced emphases of the evangelists so as to give due attention to what Francis

---

[53]   Ibid 15
[54]   *A Virtuous Church – Catholic Theology, Ethics, and Liturgy*, (Maryknoll, New York: Orbis Books, 2012), 66

J. Moloney calls 'their theologically motivated narratives'[55] and the normative implications of these narratives needs to be traced more thoroughly. The paschal morality of *Mark*, the messianic morality of *Matthew* and the merciful morality of *Luke* reflect a mosaic like pattern rather than a uniform one of New Testament moral teaching. Indeed the admission in *The Bible and Morality* that 'we cannot of course mention all models of conduct that appear in the actions and teaching of Jesus'[56] is an acknowledgement of the plurality of the ethical perspectives and presentations of the evangelists, especially the Synoptics. This also serves as a reminder to moral theologians that they are always attempting to draw 'more fully on the teaching of holy scripture'.

The biblical basis for the 'doing of theology and ethics' proceeds by taking each book – particularly the Gospels – on its own terms and interpreting them individually as an integrated narrative. Within the story that each evangelist expresses there are special emphases that suggest something of the stance of the writer and the situation of those he is writing for and to. While this avenue of exploration is partial it is necessary for historical and hermeneutical reasons given the nature of the material. The Bible is not a manual of moral theology in the manner that dominated the subject from the centuries between the Councils of Trent and Vatican II. Moral theologians have learned to handle the Bible in a spirit of humility. This has resulted in not

---

[55] *The Living Voice of the Gospel – The Gospels Today* (Dublin: Veritas, 2006), 15
[56] *The Bible and Morality*, 72

treating the Bible as a textbook or a treatise on the moral life that is timeless. The best way for moral theology to prevent itself from falling again into the fossilized form of the manuals is to begin with and go back again and again to the Bible. In the case of the New Testament this inevitably involves choosing to begin with an individual *Gospel* or *Letter*, in this case *Luke*.[57]

Luke's Diptych

Noting that tradition has handed on the image of Luke as a painter Anselm Grün states that he 'is a gifted writer who has the art of depicting things in such a way that they seem to us to be like a picture'.[58] A particular feature of his style is the 'diptych', the setting of scenes and stories, people and events side by side so that they hang like two leaves of a painting which are hinged together. The stories of the Annunciation and Visitation, the scene involving Martha and Mary, and the sight of the two thieves crucified with Jesus illustrate this method. Covering complementarity and completion, contrast and conflict the many diptychs of Luke's Gospel convey the showing of God's self-communication by Christ in history through the power of the Holy Spirit and the range of responses to the offer of salvation which these particular stories and scenes represent.

The image of a diptych also describes the interlocking of Luke's two works in the New Testament. *Gospel* and *Acts of*

---

[57] For an overview see Frank J. Matera, 'Ethics in an Age of Salvation – The Gospel according to Luke', *New Testament Ethics* (Louisville, Kentucky: Westminster John Knox Press, 1996), 64 – 91
[58] *Jesus: The Image of Humanity – Luke's Account* (London: Continuum, 2003), 13

the Apostles are like two panels that portray the story of Jesus 'the son of Adam, son of God' (Lk 3:38) and the growth of the Church among the Gentiles. While speaking of others as 'servants of the word' (Lk 1:2), Luke sets himself the double task of describing 'all that Jesus did and taught from the beginning' (Acts 1:1) and the events leading up to Paul's last two years in Rome 'proclaiming the kingdom of God and teaching about the Lord Jesus Christ' (28:31). Luke's *gospel* and *Acts* hinge on the continuity between the prophetic mission of Jesus in the power of the Spirit and the proclamation of 'repentance and forgiveness of sins in his name to all nations, beginning from Jerusalem' (Lk 24:47).[59] Changing the metaphor from painting to writing, as Luke Timothy Johnson notes, 'the hyphenated title [Luke-Acts] calls attention to the conviction that the two documents, separated in the canon by the Fourth Gospel, are two volumes of a single literary project'.[60]

Luke's 'first book' (referred to in the opening line of *Acts*) is intended to add to the other 'orderly account[s] of the events that have been fulfilled among us' (Lk 1:1). Addressing Theophilus (as he also does in *Acts*) Luke states as his purpose that 'you may know the truth concerning the things about which you have been instructed' (Lk 1:5). Reference to the many writers, 'eyewitnesses and servants of the word' who have preceded

---

[59]   Michael Mullins notes that 'there is an abundance of literary and thematic parallels between the two works'. *The Gospel of Luke* (Dublin: The Columba Press, 2010), 20. See also his *The Acts of the Apostles* (Dublin: The Columba Press, 2013)

[60]   *The Writings of the New Testament*, 3rd Edition (London: SCM Press, 2010), 187

his own publication is evidence both of earlier stages of gospel formation and Luke's own desire to contribute to the genre. The writing of a gospel was intended to preserve an account of (selected) events in the history of Jesus, including his resurrection and to present a theological interpretation of them. In addition, as Udo Schnelle states, the 'Gospels have from the pragmatic perspective an *integrative* and *innovative* function'.[61] This involves the promotion of the identity of a particular church community for '*both the church's view of itself and the ways it was regarded by outsiders*'.[62] In addition pressing issues such as separation from Judaism and internal ethical, liturgical and organizational questions shaped the narrative of each of the gospels. Luke stands out from his counterparts in having a sequel. Though they can never be separated in terms of authorship and argumentation *Luke* and *Acts* can be analysed as two distinct narratives. While *Luke* will always be related to *Acts* it can be read in its own right. As Christopher M. Tuckett states, 'the dominant trend in modern study of the Gospels has been to focus on the particularity of each Gospel and to see what that might tell us about its writer and the circumstances in which and for which it was written, quite as much as seeking to unravel the history it describes'.[63] Thus the 'particularity' of *Luke* is the subject of this study, particularly its treatment of the theme of mercy.

---

[61]   *Theology of the New Testament* (Grand Rapids, Michigan: Baker Academic, 2009), 373
[62]   Ibid, 374
[63]   *Luke* (London: T&T Clark, 2004), 13

Only Luke[64]

The BBC radio programme *Desert Island Discs* invites individuals to imagine that they are castaway and, allowed the Bible (and Shakespeare), can have only a number of selected musical pieces as well as a luxury item. Imagine instead if they could not have the whole of the Bible but only one of the gospels, and that gospel is Luke. From the Angel Gabriel's Annunciation to Mary and her Visitation of Elizabeth through the infancy narrative with its familiar items of Bethlehem, the manger and shepherds together with Mary's *Magnificat*, Zechariah's *Benedictus* and Simeon's *Nunc dimittis* the first two chapters of Luke already list many of the features that have fuelled both high art and popular culture for centuries. The Christmas story substantially follows Luke's setting and sequence of events. This dominance of detail is further reflected in the fact that, as Mullins remarks, 'one needs only to look at a list of the episodes, parables and teachings that occur in Luke to realize how the popular image of Jesus in theology, art and piety is very largely a Lucan one'.[65] Moreover, in the space of little more than a page of his *Commentary* Mullins refers to 'Luke/He alone/only' a dozen times to indicate both its individual character in terms of the Gospel tradition and its indelible contribution to Christian teaching. From beginning to end, Bethlehem to Emmaus, birth to exaltation, Luke's story of the 'Saviour, who is the Messiah, the Lord' (2:11) is vital for scholarship and spirituality in the Church. In commercial

---

[64]   *2 Timothy* 4:10

[65]   *The Gospel of Luke*, 15

terms the Lucan brand would occupy the larger share of the market in Gospel sales!

Debate about the identity of the author of this Gospel shows no sign of abating. Traditionally the author of the third Gospel – in order of appearance in the New Testament – is attributed to Luke but, as Tuckett notes, 'both the Gospel itself and Acts are anonymous'.[66] Whether the author of *Luke* and the person so named several times elsewhere in the New Testament as a member of Paul's set are one and the same involves issues which, as Tuckett claims, 'are probably of little relevance to the study of the Gospel itself'.[67] Using a metaphor in keeping with the tradition of Luke as a doctor Daniel J. Harrington's surgically states that 'this is Luke's [and] not Paul's Gospel', adding that the focus is on 'Luke's biography of Jesus, not the biography of Luke'.[68] While (other) scripture scholars (and biblical theologians) might wince at the word 'biography', Harrington's focus on the Gospel of Luke is fleshed out in the following statement of Judith Lieu: 'The perspective taken in this commentary is that to study the Gospel is not just to explore the story of Jesus of Nazareth. It is to explore *Luke's* story, to recognize how he sees Jesus both as a climax and as a beginning, to hear the voice of faith which is not the same as the voice of a documentary analysis, and so to understand how he interprets Jesus for his own time'.[69]

---

[66] *Luke,* 15

[67] Ibid, 16

[68] *Meeting St Luke Today – Understanding the Man, His Mission, and His Message* (Chicago: Loyola Press, 2009), 5

[69] *The Gospel of Luke* (Peterborough: Epworth, 1997), xiv

Moreover, the question of audience is more important than that of authorship. Identification of those Luke is addressing includes questions about Jewish and Hellenistic groupings and whether he was exclusively targeting a Gentile grouping or a mixture of contexts and congregations. Robert C. Tannehill contends that plurality and diversity were the chief characteristics of the evangelist's so-called 'target':

'These churches included people of different ethnic and religious backgrounds, social status, and wealth. There were Jews and Gentiles, women and men, poor and relatively wealthy people, common people and a few members, perhaps of the elite or retainer class who had important positions with the elite'.[70]

Contrary to the claim that Luke was addressing a completely Gentile audience, there is a growing scholarly consensus that Luke presupposes a considerable familiarity with the Hebrew scripture(s) and that both textual and theological analysis of *Luke* must take this into account:

'[Luke] goes beyond the explicit citing of scripture as proof-texts to a rich use of scripture by allusion (as in the infancy narrative). Those who do not know scripture well will not know what they are missing, for there is no citation to alert them'.[71]

---

[70]   *Luke* 24
[71]   Ibid 25-26. 'The OT functions in the writings of the Lucan evangelist in ways that are clearly distinct from the other three Gospels. He does not punctuate the tradition with proof texts as do Matthew and John; rather he punctuates his narrative with speeches that are often made up almost entirely of OT words and phrases (especially the speeches and canticles

Similarly, Stanley S. Porter sees the use of Isaiah to announce Jesus' mission at its inauguration in the synagogue at Nazareth (4:18-19) as 'a clear instance of prophetic fulfilment of the Old Testament as seen both by Luke and Jesus, and that the passage itself provides guidance to both the major themes of the Gospel and Jesus' ministry'.[72] The inclusion of both Jewish and Gentile groups and their integration in the Church is an invitation issued by Luke to experience 'salvation to the full, recognizing that God has designed both Jew and Gentile to be a part of the new community'.[73] Thus, in his geographical Gospel Luke does not set any boundaries to the embrace of God's mercy which is manifest in Jesus and maintained in the Holy Spirit to extend 'to all nations, beginning from Jerusalem' (24:47). A particular target group for this Gospel may have been the rich and wealthy. This is supported by Luke's treatment of riches and poverty which is a recurring theme of the evangelist. As Barbara Shellard notes, 'discipleship is closely connected with Luke's views on possessions/property and the importance of this theme to Luke is obvious from the full treatment he affords it'.[74] Johnson locates his language of the 'rich' and 'poor' within the overall Lucan logic of 'The Great

---

in the birth narrative). Another distinctive feature is Luke's dependence upon the LXX. Indeed, the evangelist deliberately imitates the style of the Greek OT. But this imitation does not simply involve style; it also involves substance'. Craig A. Evans, 'The Old Testament in the New', in ed Stanley L. Porter, *Hearing the Old Testament in the New Testament* (Cambridge: Eerdmans, 2006), 138-139

72   'Scripture Justifies Mission: The Use of the Old Testament in Luke-Acts' in *Hearing the Old Testament in the New Testament*, 117

73   Darrell L. Bock, 'Luke' in eds S. McKnight and Grant R. Osborne, *The Face of New Testament Studies – A Survey of Recent Research* (Grand Rapids: Baker Academic, 2004), 371

74   *New Light on Luke* (London: Sheffield Academic Press, 2002), 107

Reversal' which reveals that within the Kingdom of God there is little room for social standards of prestige, possession and power. He adds that 'the theme of reversal is expressed as well by the inclusion within the people of God of Samaritans and Gentiles'.[75] Luke's story of *Dives* (The Rich Man) and Lazarus is a powerful statement of judgement which also raises questions about the relation between justice and mercy.

Story of Salvation

Reading Luke's work backwards, that is from the end of *Acts,* his work is the story of salvation: 'Let it be known to you then that this salvation of God has been sent to the Gentiles; they will listen' (28:28). The themes of *sending* and *salvation* merge in Luke's theology of history. His account of 'salvation history' from the announcement of the angels to Zechariah and Mary through the ministry, death and resurrection of Jesus to the mission of the apostles articulates the purpose of God which was the opening of the offer of salvation to all people(s). While scholars dispute the division of Luke's depiction of the epochs of this history there is no doubt that salvation is a major theological theme of his writing. Luke Timothy Johnson states that he 'emphasizes the salvific aspect of the Good News more than any of the other Gospels'.[76] Delbert Burkett declares that 'only Luke among the evangelists refers to Jesus as a "saviour" and to his works as "salvation"'.[77] While acknowledging the

---

[75]   *The Gospel of Luke* (Collegeville, MN: The Liturgical Press, 1991), 22
[76]   Ibid, 23
[77]   'Jesus in Luke-Acts' in ed Delbert Burkett, *The Blackwell Companion to Jesus* (Oxford: Wiley-Blackwell, 2011), 47-63, here 49

difficulty of presenting an overview of Lucan theology John F. O'Grady believes that 'the Lucan theology is a theology of salvation'[78] through which 'the author presents Jesus as the bringer of salvation to the ends of the world'.[79] Focussing on both prophecy and its proclamation Luke takes a long term view in his story of salvation. O'Grady sees 'the presence of salvation' as Luke's 'principal motif'.[80] 'Motif' is a good image for indicating how Luke looks and lists the story of salvation which centres on the proclamation and presence of Jesus and will continue through the Church in the power of the Holy Spirit. Narrative is the evangelist's vehicle for expressing both the preaching and practise of Jesus which will be reflected in the words and works of the apostles. This narrative is closely connected to geography, to the unfolding of events which embrace venues ranging from Bethlehem and Galilee to Jerusalem and, in *Acts*, Damascus and Rome. Made up of many stories set in different places and involving a wide cast of characters Luke's narrative is an account of the divine salvation which has appeared in history. In the *Conclusion* of his commentary Brendan Byrne notes that most of the sixteen theses of his summary of the gospel's main ideas 'have to do with the central idea of "salvation" in Luke'.[81]

The encounter between Jesus and Zacchaeus which Luke tells of in chapter 19 shows both the style and substance of

---

[78]   *The Four Gospels and the Jesus Tradition* (New York: Paulist Press, 1989), 225

[79]   Ibid, 219

[80]   Ibid, 225

[81]   *The Hospitality of God – A Reading of Luke's Gospel* (Collegeville, MN: The Liturgical Press, 2000), 195-197

his story of salvation. In his account of the history of salvation Luke links both the panoramic and pictorial, looking at both the universal and the local. Concerned with stating that salvation should be proclaimed 'to all nations' Luke also shows that it arrives at particular locations also. Jesus tells Zacchaeus that '*today* salvation has come to this house' (19:9). The emphasis on the present here is heightened by echoing the 'today' both of Jesus' birth (2:11) and the beginning of his ministry (4:21). Referring to 'this house', Luke dovetails two of his great theological themes – Visitation and Salvation – as Jesus' presence therein proclaims the coming of salvation. The prophecy which has been fulfilled for Simeon has now also become reality for Zacchaeus and he can make his own the words, 'my eyes have seen your salvation' (2:30). The 'mighty saviour' in the 'house of David' (1:69) has brought salvation to the house of Zacchaeus 'because he too is a son of Abraham' (19:9).

For him, as with so many characters in *Luke*, salvation involves (and includes) the forgiveness of sins. This results in repentance which is realized in a range of ways, from restitution through reconciliation to the restoration of relationships. Recalling the parables of the lost sheep, coin and son(s), Jesus' closing words about coming 'to seek out and to save the lost' (19:10) communicate the compassion of God which is at the core of his mission.

Proclaiming the Prophet

Johnson states that 'in order to convey Jesus' role in God's plan for the salvation of the world, Luke draws on the image of the prophet'[82] (an interpretation supported by his analysis of the 'Prophetic Structure of Luke-Acts'[83]). Following the model of Moses, Johnson sees the prophetic pattern of the spokesman of God's word in particular socio-historical contexts who suffers and seeks divine vindication reflected in Luke's picture of Jesus. Jesus fulfils his prophetic function in word and deed, at his inaugural speech in the synagogue at Nazareth (4:16-21) and through his healing miracles and meeting outcasts and sinners. Jesus' prophetic stance is a sign of contradiction as 'those who are wealthy and powerful – represented in the story primarily by the leaders of the Jewish people – resist and reject the prophetic call to conversion'.[84] Growing resentment to Jesus results in his rejection like the prophets before him and crucifixion in Jerusalem which 'is the place of pivot in Luke's story of the Prophet and the people'.[85] Paraphrasing the cynical comments of the Jewish guards (particular to Luke's passion narrative) Jesus plays the part of the prophet in Luke's story of salvation. Within that role Jesus predicts his passion and resurrection which are fulfilled, thereby laying the foundation for the furthering of his mission by the Church in the power of the Holy Spirit. The retrospective remark of Cleopas on the road to Emmaus that 'Jesus of Nazareth was a prophet mighty in deed and word before God and all the people' places in relief the words of Hamm that he is 'a prophet and more than a

---

[82]   *Living Jesus – Learning the Heart of the Gospel* (New York: Harper San Francisco, 1999), 161
[83]   *The Gospel of Luke*, 15-20
[84]   *Living Jesus*, 166
[85]   *The Gospel of Luke*, 15

prophet'.[86] The category of 'eschatological prophet' establishes the continuity of prophesy and fulfilment in the person of Jesus the risen Lord.[87]

Using the lens of Jesus as a prophet and looking at the text and themes of the Gospel Johnson concludes:

The position that Luke's Jesus is fundamentally a prophetic figure is supported not only by multiple and converging lines of literary evidence but also by the way in which other important Lucan themes connected to Jesus are at least consonant and in most cases positively complementary to that prophetic presentation'.[88]

While there is some disagreement with Johnson's positing of the centrality of Luke's 'prophetic presentation' of the person of Jesus[89], Brian O. McDermott sees Luke depicting Jesus as 'the compassionate, Spirit-led prophet who opts for the poor, the marginalized, and the broken in mind and body'.[90] Looking

---

86   *Let the Scriptures Speak – Year C* (Collegeville, MN: The Liturgical Press, 2000), 71

87   'For [Edward] Schillebeeckx, the resurrection is the divine vindication of Jesus' life; the same people who knew him as the eschatological prophet recognized in the risen Christ the victor over death, who is thus the pledge of salvation for all who become part of his movement'. Joseph A. Fitzmyer, *Scripture & Christology – A Statement of the Biblical Commission with a Commentary* (New York: Paulist Press, 1986), 81

88   'The Christology of Luke-Acts' in eds Mark Allan Powell and David R. Bauer, *Who Do You Say That I Am?* (Louisvelle; Westminster John Knox Press, 1999), 63

89   Thus O'Toole states that '"prophet" is too narrow a concept to serve Luke for much of what he wishes to say about Jesus' - p 227. See also Burkett, footnote 4, pp 61-62

90   Brian O. McDermott, *Word Become Flesh – Dimensions of Christology* (Collegeville: Liturgical Press, 1993), 73

beyond the functional image of Jesus as prophet Luke's focus is on Jesus as the fulfilment in person of God's purpose to bring salvation to His people.

God's Travel Agent

Maurice Hogan's comment (about Mark) that 'the Christology is in the story'[91] applies *a fortiori* to Luke. The story is the key to Jesus' identity and Luke's interpretation of it. Luke gathers so many stories about journeys that scholars have come to refer to his Gospel as a travel narrative. Beginning with the angel Gabriel being 'sent by God to a town in Galilee called Nazareth' (1:26) and Mary's subsequent trip 'to a Judean town in the hill country' (1:39) to see Elizabeth Luke brings the baby Jesus 'up to Jerusalem to present him to the Lord' (2:23) and back there again 'when he was twelve years old, they went up as usual for the festival' (2:42). Geography guides the evangelist even in his account of the temptation of Jesus 'in the wilderness' as 'the devil took him to Jerusalem, and placed him on the pinnacle of the temple' (4:9). Thereafter Jesus returned to Nazareth and initiated his public ministry which involves an itinerary that is interpreted as setting 'his face to go to Jerusalem' (9:51). Raymond Brown notes that 'with his sense of theological geography, Luke calls attention to Jesus' return to Galilee and to his departure from there towards Jerusalem'.[92] The metaphor of journey underpins the story that Luke narrates. Stating that 'the *journey* is a well-known literary device found within the world of the Israelites and the people of

---

91   Quoted in Mullins, *The Gospel of Luke*, 60
92   *An Introduction to the New Testament* (New York: Doubleday, 1996), 237.

Greece and Rome' Patrick J. Hartin comments that 'The readers and hearers of Luke's gospel would have been very familiar with all these journey narratives' and that 'Luke deliberately embraces this motif'.[93]

In a work replete with many stories of memorable journeys there is one that stands out, almost serving as a gospel within the Gospel. This is the account of that made by the two who 'were going to a village called Emmaus, about seven miles from Jerusalem' (24:13). Francis J. Moloney refers to 'this unforgettable story, the subject of imaginative art, poetry, and dramatic representation across the centuries [which] retains the powerful message that lies at the heart of Luke's Gospel: despite all human sin and frailty, the kingdom of God has been definitively established through the death and resurrection of Jesus'.[94] Both in the direction they were heading and the detail of the response to the question of the Risen Jesus – 'Are you the only stranger in Jerusalem who does not know the things that have taken place there in these days?' (24:18) – Cleopas and his companion reveal that they are not going in God's way. The journey of Jesus from Galilee to Jerusalem has occupied the major part of his Gospel as the evangelist maps out what Maloney calls 'God's saving design'.[95] Transformed by Jesus' travelogue through 'all the scriptures' (24:27) and by his turning the tables on them 'when he was at table with them' (24:30) in Emmaus, the two 'returned to Jerusalem' and there 'told what

---

[93]   *Exploring the Spirituality of the Gospels* (Collegeville, MN: 2011), 48-49

[94]   *The Resurrection of the Messiah*, (New York: Paulist Press, 2013), 86

[95]   Ibid, 82

had happened on the road, and how he had been made known to them in the breaking of the bread' (24:35). By retracing the steps of Jesus Luke records the story of salvation which 'is to be proclaimed in his name to all nations, beginning from Jerusalem' (24:49).

Gospel of God's Mercy

Gentleness and graciousness are often mentioned as two of the characteristic qualities of *Luke*. Looking at the three year cycle of the Sunday Lectionary Normand Bonneau states that 'Luke's special material sketches the portrait of a God of inexhaustible and overwhelming graciousness'.[96] In his letter to Luke Albino Luciani/Pope John Paul I begins by stating 'I've always liked you! You were all gentleness'.[97] The renowned biblical scholar Raymond Brown remarks that 'accurately Dante described him as "the scribe of the gentleness of Christ" – more than any other evangelist Luke has given the world a Jesus to love'.[98] Luke lets mercy guide his gospel, governing the encounters he describes throughout so that 'the God of Israel and of Luke's narrative is gracious and merciful, boundless in generosity towards the people'.[99] The graciousness of God and the gentleness of Christ are grounded in the divine mercy.

---

[96] 'Luke's Distinctive Sunday Lectionary Profile', *The Bible Today*, 38(2000):337-342, here 341

[97] *Illustrissimi – The Letters of Pope John Paul I* (London: Collins, 1976), 217

[98] *An Introduction to the New Testament*, 267

[99] 'The God of Israel and the Salvation of the Nations', in Eds A. Andrew Das and Frank J. Matera, *The Forgotten God – Perspectives in Biblical Theology* (Louisville: Westminster John Knox Press, 2002): 91-105, here 105

John Navone identifies *Mercy* as one of twenty themes 'of the Third Gospel', arguing that 'the examination of many distinct themes, despite their frequent overlapping, favours an appreciation of Lucan theology which is more analytic than synthetic'.[100] Following Jacques Dupont, Navone notes that 'in speaking of the mercy of God, the Bible frequently joins "merciful" (*eleeson*) with "compassionate" (*oiktirmon*): "God is compassionate and merciful", concluding that 'mercy and compassion (loving-kindness) are pre-eminently divine attributes'.[101] Turning to the New Testament, Navone states that 'the meaning of the divine mercy finds expression throughout Luke's Gospel'.[102] Linking mercy with the Lucan theme of universalism, he underscores that 'it is Jesus who reveals the goodness and mercy of God in its fullness'.[103] In a summary statement Wilfrid J. Harrington asserts that 'at any rate the Christ of Luke is throughout, and before all else, a Saviour who is full of compassion and tenderness and great forgiveness'.[104]

Notwithstanding Navone's preference for analysis over synthesis (though it is surprising that, unlike Harrington, he does not list *Forgiveness* among the themes of *Luke*) this study will

---

[100] *Themes of St Luke* (Rome: Gregorian University Press, 1970), 9. The other themes identified by Navone number *Banquet, Conversion, Faith, Fatherhood, Grace, Jerusalem, Joy, Kingship, Must, Poverty, Prayer, Prophet, Salvation, Spirit, Temptation, Today, Universalism, Way, Witness*

[101] Ibid, 96

[102] Ibid, 97

[103] Ibid, 98. See also his 'The Compassion of Jesus in the Synoptics', *The Bible Today*, 40 (July/August 2002): 242-247

[104] *The Gospel according to St Luke* (London: Geoffrey Chapman, 1968), 21-22

focus on the evangelist's exposition of mercy as the field force which reveals the manifestation of God's compassion in the course and conduct of Jesus' ministry, death and resurrection that is to be continued through 'all generations' (1:48) and 'proclaimed in his name to all nations' (24:47) in the power of the Holy Spirit. Guided by the concluding comment of John T. Carroll that 'the reader of Luke's narrative cannot separate its theological convictions and ethical vision'[105], the following chapters are constructed on the foundation of Harrington's claim that 'the gospel of Luke is a gospel of mercy'.[106] Combining theology with geography, Luke creates a theo-graphy of mercy throughout his gospel.

---

[105] 'The Gospel of Luke: A Contemporary Cartography', *Interpretation*, 68 (2014): 366-375, here 375
[106] *The Gospel according to St Luke*, 22

Chapter Three

Mercy From On High

'Luke shapes the contours of the Christ event in his own distinctive manner. The canticles of Mary and Zechariah, couched in the rhythmic cadences of the psalms, resonate with the gracious mercy and compassion of God. Compassion motivates God's entry into human history and moves Jesus to the side of those suffering. While Matthew has, "Be perfect, as your heavenly Father is perfect", Luke writes simply, "Be merciful, even as your Father is merciful". Mercy and compassion when received and when extended to others bring people into the family of God... In his ministry, as presented by Luke, Jesus is himself "the compassion of God", showing compassion to those in need and telling parables where through compassion people become bearers of God's mercy and love'.[107]

There are five references to mercy in the first chapter of *Luke*. As Darrell L. Bock notes, 'God as merciful is stressed in the infancy material (1:50, 54, 58, 72, 78)'[108]. The first two appear in *Mary's*

---

[107] John R. Donahue, *The Gospel in Parable* (Minneapolis: Fortress Press, 1988), 211

[108] *A Theology of Luke and Acts* (Grand Rapids, Michigan: Zondervan, 2012), 262

Song of Praise while the final two are found in *Zechariah's Song*. The third mention of mercy is situated between the stories of Mary and Elizabeth and, while directly related to the joyful delivery of John, could also serve as a commentary on the conception (and birth) of Mary's child: 'Her neighbours and relatives heard that the Lord had shown his great mercy to her, and they rejoiced with her' (1:58). The addition of 'great' to the other attributions of God's mercy augments the awareness of joy which 'is, in Luke, a characteristic of faith that recognizes salvation history marching forward'.[109] The evangelist's method and message are made clear from the beginning, in the diptych of the angel Gabriel's appearances to Zechariah and Mary and in the articulation of their acknowledgement of salvation history through their respective sons, John and Jesus.

Revelation and Response

Luke's version of the Infancy Narrative is viewed primarily through the diptych of Zechariah/John and Mary/Jesus.[110] The angel's appearance is the divine answer to the intercession of Zechariah. Identifying himself as Gabriel, the heavenly messenger reveals that he has 'been sent to speak and bring you this good news' (1:19). This proclamation pertains to the conception of the child who, following in the prophetic tradition of Israel, will precede Jesus and prepare a people turned towards the Lord through conversion. The second panel of this diptych shifts the scene from the temple in Jerusalem to

---

[109]   François Bovon, *Luke 1* (Minneapolis: Fortress Press, 2002), 70
[110]   For a detailed study of the *Lucan Infancy Narrative* see Raymond E. Brown, *The Birth of The Messiah* (London: Geoffrey Chapman, 1978)

the town of Bethlehem in Galilee. The parallel appearance of Gabriel to Mary allows for both continuity and discontinuity, prophecy and fulfilment. While Zechariah's incredulity initially falls short of the mark and incurs the (temporary) loss of speech, he will more than make up in the eloquence of his *Benedictus*, Luke interestingly places Mary's prayer, the *Magnificat*, before Zechariah's. Commenting on the *Magnificat*, *Benedictus* (and *Nunc Dimittis* of Simeon), Brown concludes that

> The most satisfactory solution is that the canticles were composed in a non-Lucan circle and that originally they praised the salvific action of God without any precise reference to the events that Luke was narrating in the infancy narrative. Nevertheless, when Luke considered these canticles, he saw how they might be brought into the infancy narrative with relatively little adaptation. The piety and the concept of salvation found in the canticles correspond well to the piety and the concept of salvation that one could expect from the main figures of the infancy narrative.[111]

The *Annunciation*, as the story of Gabriel's invitation and Mary's response is traditionally termed, is the subject and source of much artistic inspiration and industry.[112] Their encounter and exchange express and embody the Gospel. Mary is made to conceive from heaven rather than humanly. A profusion of titles portends the mission of her son and her indispensable

---

[111] Ibid, 349
[112] For an account of this and also of the historical and cultural setting of the story of the Annunciation see Kathleen Coyle, 'And the Angel Left Her', *Doctrine & Life*, 61(December 2011): 5-16

acceptance according to the word of God announced by the angel. The 'proof' of this prophecy is provided by the promise of Elizabeth's conception of John and the account of Mary's journey to visit Elizabeth who confirms and completes the activity of the Holy Spirit in responding to the coming of her cousin. Mary, who has earlier stated that she saw herself as 'servant of the Lord' (1:38) is now (and henceforth) greeted as 'the mother of my Lord' (1:43). This verbal diptych dovetails the dynamic of revelation and response with the divine designation of Mary's child as *Lord* (Luke's 'most characteristic title for Jesus and his favourite address to him'[113]) and the description of her discipleship in terms of the service of maternity for a child 'who will be great, and will be called the Son of the Most High' (1:32).

Magnifying God's Mercy

Commentary on Mary's Canticle often commences with comparison with the hymn of Miriam in *Exodus* (15:1-18).[114] The sense of continuity is significant as her first reference to God's mercy recalls the faithful love that God has consistently shown. Linguistically this is reflected in the use of *eleos* which, as Brown notes 'is the normal rendition of the Hebrew *hesed*, God's covenantal love in choosing Israel (or David) as a covenant partner without merit on the people's part'.[115] Elena Bosetti brings out this connection:

---

[113] Eric Franklin, *Luke*, in eds John Muddiman and John Barton, *The Gospels – The Oxford Bible Commentary*, (Oxford: Oxford University Press, 2010 updated), 135

[114] See Reid, *Choosing the Better Part?*, 76

[115] *The Birth of the Messiah*, 337

The Magnificat sings the story of divine mercy, which bestows itself in many forms: towards the mothers of Israel and towards their sons, in fidelity to the promise made to their father Abraham, in whose name the canticle closes. Mercy, the divine *eleos,* is therefore the guiding theme of the Magnificat, the golden thread [of mercy] that connects Mary's situation to that of Israel.[116]

Moreover, with a focus on the future – 'Surely, from now on all generations will call me blessed' (1:48) – there is hope of closure in the sense of completion of the covenant. The remembrance of God's mercy (1:54) connects past, present and future through her reference 'to our ancestors, to Abraham and to his descendants forever' (1:55). Richard J. Dillon remarks that 'indeed, Scripture argues in the *Magnificat* all the way from the "mercy" shown to Mary to the "mercy" shown to Abraham – thus, from the preternatural virginal conception to the emergence of Mary's people, Abraham's heirs'.[117] Promise and fulfilment coalesce in Mary's canticle as the kingdom that her child will inaugurate and incarnate has, as Gabriel informed her, no end. Echoing 'the *Magnificat's* reference to the endless mercy of God', Brown states that 'the salvation that has come in Jesus of Nazareth is the definitive act by which God has kept his covenant with Israel, the ultimate manifestation of His mercy (covenant kindness) to His servant people'.[118]

---

[116]   *Luke – The Song of God's Mercy* (Boston, MA: Pauline, 2006), 36

[117]   *The Hymns of Saint Luke – Lyricism and Narrative Strategy in Luke 1-2,* (Washington, DC: The Catholic Biblical Association of America, 2013), 47-48

[118]   Ibid, 364

The *Magnificat* links the human experience of salvation with the divine manifestation of mercy. Mercy is not simply a synonym for salvation but its source. Mercy is the motive for God's reaching out through the ages. Beginning with Abraham, God's mercy 'is for those who fear him from generation to generation' and it will extend to the ends of the earth (as Luke will endeavour to express in his *Gospel* and *Acts*). This is the universality of God's mercy. Intended for all people, Mary accepts her humble part in its mission and articulates her awareness that the scope of God's saving mercy is the fulfilment of promises 'made to our ancestors' (1:55). God's 'mercy for those who fear him' has important implications in the area of justice involving the vindication of the poor and lowly and, inversely, the vilification of the rich, proud and powerful. The consequence of this contrast between the humble and haughty is captured in. Dillon's declaration:

> The clash of these responses, the responsive and the recusant, is portrayed again in the familiar language the Hebrew Bible applied to God's friends and opponents, typically fated to act out a wholesale *reversal of fortunes* under the impact of God's mighty deed for Jesus' mother.[119]

Liberation theologians in particular point to the *Magnificat* as a pivotal text for both understanding and undertaking the praxis of justice as a core constituent of Christian faith and participation in the transformation of the world. Alfred T. Hennelly articulates this Marian underpinning of action for justice:

---

[119] *Hymns of Saint Luke*, 33

We see that the key to liberation Mariology is discovered through a careful analysis of the gospel of Luke. The salient text, not unexpectedly, turns out to be the *Magnificat*, where God intervenes to overthrow the power of the mighty and to exalt those of low status.[120]

Glorifying God's Mercy

True to its word Zechariah's *Song of Praise* prepares the way for the Lord as it precedes the account of Jesus' birth. In this way Luke literally highlights the representative (of Israel) and revelatory (of Jesus) role of Elizabeth and Zechariah's son. Quoting Isaiah, the focus of John is on the figure of Jesus as the fulfilment of the Messianic promise that 'all flesh shall see the salvation of God' (3:6). Seeing that 'salvation has come to the Gentiles in the message about Jesus' Bock states that 'from the first of Luke to the last of Acts, God's saving activity is in view'.[121] As though taking a clue from Mary's praise of God as Saviour, Zechariah proclaims that God 'has raised up a mighty saviour for us in the house of his servant David' (1:69) and points to David's descendant as the 'prophet of the Most High' who will 'give knowledge of salvation to his people by the forgiveness of their sins' (1:76-77). The invitation to redemption and response of repentance represent the divine and human sides of salvation and, as such, reflect what François Bovon calls 'the theological structure of the indicative and imperative

---

[120]   *Liberation Theologies – The Global Pursuit of Justice* (Mystic, CT: Twenty-Third Publications, 1995) 63. See also Donal Dorr, 'A Biblical Example' in *Spirituality and Justice* (Maryknoll, NY: Orbis Books, 198), 36-40

[121]   *A Theology of Luke and Acts*, 259-260

in [verses] 73b-75'.[122] The experience of redemption both engenders and expects a moral response. Being 'rescued from the hands of enemies' enables service of God 'without fear, in holiness and righteousness before him all our days' (1:75). This service reaches out to others in remembrance of God's mercy.

The first (of two) references in the *Benedictus* to God's mercy relates it to the fulfilment of promise(s) and the furtherance of the covenant: 'He has shown the mercy promised to our ancestors, and has remembered his holy covenant' (1:72). This showing of God's mercy is seen in its performance as a concrete and contemporaneous activity. The combination of mercy and memory in the context of the covenant is a confirmation of the continuity of God's choice and commitment to the salvation of His people. Joel Green highlights the centrality of mercy in Luke's composition:

> The mention of God's mercy appearing near the middle of this first major segment of the Song (vv 68-75) is pivotal. Here we find the fundamental basis for God's behaviour in any time, and it is surely significant that Jesus will later identify mercy as the primary motivation behind God's activity and as the basis for the ethical behaviour for the community of disciples. This mercy is active: literally, God has "done mercy".[123]

This is reinforced by the (second) reference to 'the tender mercy of our God' (1:78). Brown translates this as 'heartfelt

---

[122]   *Luke 1*, 75
[123]   *The Gospel of Luke* (Eerdmans: Cambridge, U.K., 1997), 117

mercy', taking the Greek *splanchna* as indicating 'the innermost parts of mercy'.[124] Green maintains that 'the manifestation of God's mercy according to the *Song* is the coming of the Messiah'.[125] Interpreting the mystery of God's motivation in terms of 'tender mercy' is testified in the graciousness and generosity of divine dealings with Mary, Elizabeth and Zechariah (and subsequently in the infancy sequence with Simeon and Anna) and, in turn, in the way these parents and persons treat their respective children, John and Jesus. John T. Carroll comments that 'the singer ascribes the advent of deliverance for the people, and the particular roles of John and Jesus, to divine mercy' and that 'also stemming from this divine mercy will be a visit from a dawn from on high'.[126] Thus the exposition of God's mercy is expressed in the effect of light extinguishing darkness. The emergence of a new day, 'the dawn from on high' which 'will break upon us' (1:78), enables light to enter into the lives of 'those who sit in darkness and in the shadow of death' (1:79). This light will lead both the people of Israel and the Gentiles 'into the way of peace' (1:79). This metaphor for salvation is picked up by Simeon in his reference to 'a light for revelation to the Gentiles and for glory to your people Israel' (2:32). The angels attested to the advent of peace among those favoured by God. Simeon himself is the first to fully enjoy this mercy of God as he is dismissed in peace and departs this world for eternal life.

---

[124]   *The Birth of the Messiah*, 373
[125]   *The Gospel of Luke*, 119
[126]   *Luke – A Commentary* (Louisville, Kentucky:Westminster John Knox Press, 2012), 61

Perfecting God's Mercy

Mullins calls the Sermon on the Plain 'Luke's loose "parallel" to Matthew's Sermon on the Mount'.[127] It's content (6:20-49) is much shorter than the three chapters Matthew devotes to Jesus' moral teaching.[128] Though sometimes described as a scaled down version of the Sermon on the Mount consideration must also be given to the special features of the Sermon on the Plain and the fact that 'much of the teaching which Matthew includes... is located by Luke in Jesus' teaching on the way to Jerusalem as recounted in Lk 9:51-19:27)'.[129] A significant difference in the setting of the two 'Sermons' lies in Luke's listing of the audience to include 'a great multitude of people from all Judaea, Jerusalem, and the coast of Tyre and Sidon' (6:17). This detail could be interpreted as an expression of the extension of Jesus' ethic through the expansion of the ecclesial community.

The Sermon on the Plain begins (like the Sermon on the Mount) with the Beatitudes, though Luke limits his list to four, followed by four corresponding Woes. For Matthew the Beatitudes are more than a mere preface, they are a prologue to what follows. The key to interpreting and integrating them with the rest of the Sermon on the Mount lies in the lines that

---

[127] *The Gospel of Luke*, 212. For a detailed commentary see L. John Topel, Children of a Compassionate God – A Theological Exegesis of Luke 6:20-49 (Collegeville, Minnesota: The Liturgical Press, 2001)

[128] For an account and analysis see my 'Matthew's Messianic Morality', *Doctrine & Life*, 59 (January 2009): 36-47

[129] *The Gospel of Luke*, 212. For a graphic comparison of the two 'sermons' see Ben Witherington III, *The Indelible Image – The Theological and Ethical Thought World of the New Testament, Volume One* (Downers Grove, Illinois: IVP Academic, 2009), 703

immediately follow them, the images of salt and light that indicate the necessity of grace, of receiving before responding, of a foundation for building on. The loss of taste, hiding the light and constructing on sand rather than stone (7:24-27) are frightening indications of the fallout from lack of listening to and living the word of God which is authoritatively taught by Jesus. As symbols of blandness, blindness and bad building they show the state of sin, that is alienation from God and that leads to damnation. For Matthew the Beatitudes do not function as a form of reward or a *do ut des* exchange[130], that is, giving in order to gain in return. Instead the invitation to enter into the Kingdom of Heaven is to receive the gift of righteousness that is revealed as grace. To respond to this call is to be rooted in the Gospel and to bear the fruits of faithful living. The Beatitudes are – literally – blessings which provide a basis for growth in goodness and holiness.

Luke's method of juxtaposing the Beatitudes and the Woes is a powerful literary device which reflects commendation or condemnation for the choices (and their consequences) that people make. Reflecting the author's option for the poor and opposition to those who trust in their present possession of material goods, this method of contrast confirms the promises proclaimed in the *Magnificat*. To adapt another Lucan phrase the 'better part' will be reserved for those who keep faith in God and follow the Son of Man. Thus 'the Beatitudes and Woes

---

130   The phrase is taken from Jean-Louis Souletie, 'Which Christological Tools for the Interreligious Dialogue', in eds Lieven Boeve, Frederiek Depoortere and Spephan Van Erp, *Edward Schillebeeckx and Contemporary Theology* (London: T & T Clark, 2010), 98-108, here 106

continue the Lucan literary pattern of reversal' whereby 'instead of speaking of internal dispositions which yield specific results (as in Matthew), Luke describes objective conditions that will be or are being reversed by God'.[131]

The Beatitude which Matthew presents as his fifth, 'Blessed are the merciful, for they will receive mercy' (5:7), is not replicated in Luke. Notwithstanding questions of sources and issues of interaction (and interpretation) between the evangelists, this omission seems surprising given his earlier choice of mercy as constituting a core meaning for the community in communicating and continuing the mission of Jesus. Luke's invocation of mercy is integral to his theological intention to inculcate it as a virtue both in those who 'had come to hear him' (6:18) and those who would hear the word of God through their words, works and witness. Guessing the mind of an evangelist runs the risk of taking his imagination for granted, to say nothing of the inspiration of the Holy Spirit. However, whatever his editorial motivation, Luke may have considered it superfluous to specify mercy as a particular beatitude or unnecessary to underline it. The four beatitudes identified by Luke involve states or situations – poverty and hunger, weeping and being hated by others – which have not been chosen and over which those subject to them have no control. Luke mentions mercy in his 'sermon' – 'Be merciful, just as your Father is merciful'(6:36) – and this call comes as a completion of Jesus' teaching placed in the text after the Beatitudes and Woes. Thus Léopold Sabourin comments that 'the call to be 'merciful' comes in the context of

---

131   *Luke*, 111

Luke in an appropriate way, at the same time to conclude the preceding exposition on love of enemies and to introduce the new section on mercy'.[132]

Prior to this concentration on mercy Luke sets out a number of other commandments. These are bracketed within the double reference to 'love your enemies' (6:27, 35).[133] Charity towards those 'who hate you' contains the general norm to 'do good' to them which is spelt out in a number of specific challenges: returning blessing and prayer for those who curse and abuse, turning the other cheek to those who strike, giving goods away and not asking for them in return. This 'reckless generosity'[134] seems difficult to reconcile with Luke's restatement of the *Golden Rule* – 'Do to others as you would have them do to you' (6:31) – with its rule of reciprocity.[135] However, he goes beyond a morality based on mutuality of respect in rejecting relationships based on receiving in return, rejecting an ethic of parity with the threefold repetition of the rhetorical question 'what credit is that to you?' and reiterating that even sinners do as much. The disciples are to do good, lend to others and love,

---

[132] *L'évangile de Luc – Introduction et Commentaire* (Roma: Editrice Pontificia Universita Gregoriana, 1987), 165 (My translation)

[133] For a detailed discussion of this commandment see Boivon, *Luke 1*, 234-239

[134] This phrase is taken from Frank O'Connor, *An Only Child* (London: Macmillan & Co Ltd, 1965), 137

[135] 'Some philologists recognize an absolute criticism of every form of reciprocity in Jesus' ethics. They claim either that the Golden Rule was taken up only later by Christian ethics, or that the original version of the Sermon on the Plain directly negates its content; this latter hypothesis is, however, only possible with the acceptance of an emendation of the text'. *Luke 1*, 240

even enemies, 'expecting nothing in return' (6:35). However, in the same sentence Luke states that such dispositions and deeds will be rewarded, which 'will be great', that is, to be designated as 'children of the Most High'. Recalling the description of John the Baptist as a 'child [who] will be called the prophet of the Most High' (1:76 discipleship is defined in terms of duplication of the kindness of God who does not distinguish between those who are generous or grudging, warmhearted or wicked. The designation of God as the 'Most High' shows that His dealings with people derive from a different level, that 'God in His generosity is going to recompense the generous man with a divine measure incomparably greater than human measure'.[136] Such generosity reflects that 'God's mercy is, finally, why compassion and mercy extend even to enemies, and that is why one refrains from judging another'.[137]

Luke's list of teachings about love – especially of enemies – lending without hope of return and living like children of God leads him to the *law of mercy*: 'Be merciful, just as your Father is merciful' (6:36). Green interprets this intimate relation as requiring that 'just as God is merciful – that is, just as God is active graciously and creatively to bring about redemption – so should His children be merciful'.[138] Where Luke mandates mercy, Matthew prescribes perfection: 'Be perfect, therefore, as your heavenly Father is perfect' (5:48). Boivon states that these sayings 'hint at the rare Hebrew Bible theologoumenon of the *imitatio Dei*' and have different functions for the two evangelists,

---

[136]   *L'évangile de Luc*, 166
[137]   Carroll, *Luke – A Commentary*, 152
[138]   *The Gospel of Luke*, 275

'a parenetic function in Matthew [which] in Luke receives the role of a theological justification'.[139] Matthew's exhortation to imitate the perfection of the heavenly Father is not the expression of an impossible ideal but rather an invitation to become, in the words of Frank Matera, 'whole, entire, undivided in allegiance and devotion to God'.[140] Thus imitation of the divine generosity will issue from identification with God and insertion into the life of grace. According to Boivon, 'of the two main attributes of God, His compassion and His holiness, Luke chooses compassion as the fount of Christian behaviour'.[141]

In describing the limitless demands of mercy for the disciples Luke is at the same time not declaring the impossibility of imitating the divine measure of dealing with people. Mindful of Gabriel's encouragement to Mary that 'nothing will be impossible with God' (1:37), Luke looks to the perfection of God's mercy in history through the disciples drawing from the depths of its divine well. In proclaiming mercy as the supreme standard and source of the Christian moral life Luke is pointing out not only its theological understanding but also its spiritual underpinning. For Luke 'the divine perfection that the disciples are to imitate is the perfection of an all-embracing mercy'.[142] Moreover, he shows how mercy is to be undertaken by the family of God through the practices and pronouncements of Jesus, the prophet of the Father's mercy.

---

[139]   *Luke 1*, 241
[140]   *The Sermon on the Mount* (Collegeville, MN: The Liturgical Press, 2013), 64
[141]   *Luke 1*, 241
[142]   Justo L. González, *Luke* (Louisville, Kentucky: Westminster John Knox Press, 2010), 94

Miracles Of Mercy

'Luke's Gospel is most concerned with Jesus' true humanity and his compassion for the outcasts of society. Only in Luke does Jesus cleanse the Samaritan leper. He is also interested in portraying Jesus as Saviour of the world. Part of the holistic salvation which Jesus brings includes physical healing'.[143]

The Man of Mercy

The first of the miracles in Luke in which mercy is mentioned is the story of the raising to life of the widow's son at Nain (7: 11-17). Giving the barest details about the funeral scene Jesus encountered on his entry into the town - constituted by the dead man who was an only son of his widowed mother and the large cortege that accompanied them – Luke states that 'when the Lord saw her, he had compassion for her and said to her, "Do not weep"'. Motivated by mercy, Jesus moves towards the bier and after touching it says to the young man 'I say to you, rise!' After the dead man returns to life and responds with speech the evangelist adds poignantly that 'Jesus gave him to his mother'.

---

[143]   C.L. Blomberg (noted American scholar of the New Testament), 'Healing', in eds Joel B. Green and Scot McKnight, *Dictionary of Jesus and the Gospels* (Leicester, England: InterVarsity Press, 1992), 299-307, here 303

The remainder of the story is taken up by the reaction of the crowd and how this 'word about him [Jesus] spread throughout Judea and all the surrounding country'. Fred B. Craddock gives a moving account of the story of the widow's son:

'This episode offers a dramatic example of Jesus' ministry of compassion. The object of his compassion is the mother. His total attention is on this woman who is a widow and whose only son, her sole means of support as well as being her whole family, is dead. There is sadness enough when children bury parents, but it does not compare to the grief attending nature's reversal, when parents bury children. Jesus' whole attention is on the woman; the storyteller seems unaware of the disciples, the crowd, the bearers, the mourners. Jesus acts without drama, ritual, or even prayer'.[144]

This miracle story manifests many of the moral and theological concerns of Luke. Like the other widows in *Luke* – one who persists in asking (and annoying) the unjust judge until she gets her due (18:2-5) and the other observed giving all she had left to the treasury (21:1-4) – the woman in this story is another anonymous figure among the socially marginalized. The evangelist's concern covers not only her economic situation but also her emotional state. This widow's destitution is deepened in every way by the death of her only son. Seeing her plight, Jesus is moved to the core of his being. Johnson notes that the verb for 'he felt compassion' indicates

---

[144] *Luke* (Louisville, Kentucky: John Knox Press, 1990), 96-97

'the inner emotion accompanying mercy'.[145] Albert Nolan's analysis accentuates the intensity of this emotion and the extent of Jesus' involvement:

> The English word 'compassion' is far too weak to express the emotion that moved Jesus. The Greek verb *splagchnizomai* used is derived from the noun *splagchnon*, which means intestines, bowels, entrails or heart, that is to say, the inner parts of one's system from which strong emotions seem to arise. The Greek verb therefore means a movement or impulse that wells up from one's very entrails, a gut reaction. That is why English translators have to resort to expressions like 'he was moved with compassion or pity' or 'he felt sorry' or 'his heart went out to them'. But even these do not capture the deep physical and emotional flavour of the Greek word for compassion'.[146]

Giving her situation due consideration shows that 'the praxis of Jesus reveals a particular care and concern for the needs of the person in front of him'.[147] The importance of sight is indicated in two other instances in Chapter 7 of *Luke*. On both occasions Jesus is speaking, firstly to the two disciples sent by John the Baptist to enquire whether he was the Messiah, secondly to Simon the Pharisee who had invited him to dine with him. Telling the two disciples to 'Go and tell John what you have seen (and heard)' (7:22), Jesus testifies to the fulfilment of

---

[145]   *The Gospel of Luke*, 118
[146]   *Jesus before Christianity* (Maryknoll, NY: Orbis Books, 1988), 28
[147]   Wayne Morris, *Salvation as Praxis* (London: Bloomsbury, 2014), 141

the text of Isaiah which he read from at the inauguration of his mission in Nazareth. Asking Simon 'Do you see this woman?' (7:44), Jesus is referring to the 'woman in the city, who was a sinner' who came and washed his feet with her tears and wiped them with her hair. This question is not a matter of merely recognizing or identifying this – in contrast to Simon – unnamed woman but rather a rhetorical device. Pointing to the depth of her faith Jesus proclaims forgiveness of her and her sins. Linked to the earlier line about the Lord seeing the widow in Nain Luke sets Jesus' looking at people in the perspective of salvation. The merciful gaze of Jesus is the manifestation of God's power for salvation.

Gerhard Lohfink states that Jesus did not consider his miraculous activity as separate from his message but that both words and deeds should be seen as of a piece, proclaiming and making present God's Kingdom in the power of the Spirit:

> So Jesus did not regard the saving deeds he performed as isolated authenticating miracles. His deeds of power had a different origin and goal. They arose out of the crisis, the need he encountered on all sides, and they are the beginning of the new world God is giving. They are signs of the inbreaking reign of God. They are signs that now the Old Testament prophecies are being fulfilled. Hence Jesus' mighty deeds stand within a referential context that itself makes them what they are. There is absolutely no

comparable framework for the miracles otherwise reported in antiquity.[148]

To illustrate this unique framework for interpreting the miracles of Jesus Lohfink compares the miracle at Nain with the story by Philostratus of Apollonius of Tyana's raising of a young girl from the dead.[149] There are many similarities in both stories: the dead person is young, the grieving are supported by the community, Apollonius and Jesus are both depicted as displaying compassion, previous accounts are pointed to, 'of Alcestis by the demigod Heracles, while [Luke] uses a literary reference to recall the raising of the son of the widow of Zarephath by the prophet Elijah'.[150] However, the dissimilarities between the two stories are determinative:

> Apollonius' miracle-working words are magical. Philostratus does not want to say it too directly, but that is the precise background. Jesus, in contrast, does

---

148 *Jesus of Nazareth – What He Wanted, Who He Was*, Collegeville, MN: Liturgical Press, 2012, 147. For a summary of the treatment of Jesus' miracles and their meaning by scripture scholars, see Michael J. Daling and Christopher M. Hays, 'The historical Jesus' in eds Christopher M. Hays and Christopher B. Ansberry, *Evangelical Faith and the Challenge of Historical Criticism* (London: SPCK, 2013), 158-181, especially 165-170.

149 Lohfink lists the following details: 'Apollonius, an itinerant philosopher, lived between 40 and 120 CE. He was regarded in antiquity as a preacher and a miracle worker. He is supposed to have forged amulets that protected against earthquake, wind, water, mosquitoes, and mice. We have scarcely any truly reliable sources regarding his teaching and life. Over a hundred years later Philostratus was encouraged by the Roman empress Julia Domna to write a novelistic description of his life that in many respects reads like an "anti-gospel". As part of his *Vita*, Philostratus tells the following story'. *Jesus of Nazareth*, 147

150 Ibid 149

not utter any words of wizardry but speaks a very brief command: "Rise!" Further, Philostratus insinuates that the girl only appeared to be dead. A further difference in the story is the role of God...But the *decisive* difference is that Philostratus portrays Apollonius as an effective and humane miracle worker...in reality it is all about Apollonius, and the whole event, despite the sorrow of the city of Rome over the young woman, remains a private matter. It is just the reverse in Luke: here it is all about Israel.[151]

The background to the story of the widow's son at Nain in *I Kings 17* with its account of the prophet Elijah restoring a dead child to life and to his poverty stricken mother intensifies both the drama and the disclosure of God's intervention in Jesus. Reference to the body of bystanders declaring that 'a great prophet has risen among us' (7:16) allows Luke to make his first 'explicit application of the title prophet to Jesus in the narrative, although Jesus' prophetic ministry has been abundantly demonstrated'.[152] For Green this miracle means that 'more than a prophet, Jesus is the compassionate benefactor of the poor'.[153] Added to this declaration is the assertion that 'God has looked favourably on his people' (7:16), representing visitation as the pre-eminent form of God's revelation which establishes relations of hospitality and healing. C. Kavin Rowe remarks that this declaration 'is coordinated with Zechariah's

---

[151] Ibid (Lohfink states that he is 'setting aside all historical questions!' in his comparison of the two stories.)

[152] Johnson, *The Gospel of Luke*, 119

[153] *The Gospel of Luke*, 290

prophecy in Luke 1 in such a way as to give implicit unity to the action of Jesus and the God of Israel at the point of the power of their compassion'.[154] The evangelist's expressive introduction of Jesus as 'the Lord' reinforces this idea of divine activity.[155] Lohfink links the fate of the individual with that of Israel:

> It is not only that God Himself has acted in Jesus to raise up the young man of Nain! Still more, God has acted in Israel, his people. This theological interpretation of the event is breathtaking. What has happened in the little village of Nain, and for one widow, is applied to all Israel. The miracle story opens a vista onto a long history of God's promises and mighty deeds in Israel. Therefore Jesus' mercy shown to the widow is not mere human sympathy as with Apollonius, but a reflection of God's mercy on His people.[156]

A fascinating feature of this story is that it contains no reference to faith. Luke sets it between the stories of the healing of the seriously ill slave of the Roman centurion and the forgiveness of her sins for the woman who washed the feet of Jesus with her tears and dried them with her hair. The first story evokes Jesus' encomium 'I tell you, not even in Israel have I

---

[154] *Early Narrative Christology – The Lord in the Gospel of Luke* (Grand Rapids, Michigan: Baker Academic, 2006), 121

[155] Ben Witherington III notes that *kyrios* 'is by far the most frequently used title in all of Luke-Acts' and that 'the basic concept Luke has of *kyrios* seems to be one who exercises dominion over the world, and particularly over human lives and events'. *The Many Faces of the Christ – The Christologies of the New Testament and Beyond* (New York: Crossroad, 1998), 158

[156] *Jesus of Nazareth*, 150

found such faith' (7:9) while the latter ends with the elaboration 'Your faith has saved you' (7:50). Moreover, Luke does not place faith as the foundation for the prophetic identification of Jesus and the pronouncement of God's presence but the fact that 'fear seized all of them; and they glorified God' (7:16). Omission of a(ny) reference to faith in the story of the raising of the widow's son at Nain fixes the focus firmly on Jesus, on his motivation and manifestation of God's mercy. The seemingly simple words - 'When the Lord saw her, he had compassion for her' – support the weight of the Gospel and state the working of God's mercy in and through Jesus, the prophet of God's presence.[157] Byrne brings out the essence of the encounter where 'Nothing is said about her faith, and in this respect the young man, too, is necessarily passive. The episode simply instances

---

[157] After a detailed discussion of what he calls 'the Nain story' John P. Meier concludes: 'It is interesting to note that, when weighing his decision, [Gerard] Rochais points out that the concrete location of Nain is one of the most serious arguments in favour of historicity. In fact, in my opinion, Rochais never does give an adequate explanation of how the name of this obscure town became attached to what he sees as a Christian reworking of the Elijah story in I Kings 17. To this concrete nugget of the town's name there may be added a much more general observation: the various sources of the canonical Gospels do not show any tendency or interest in multiplying miracle stories in which Jesus raises from the dead. The Marcan, Lucan, and Johannine traditions each knew of only one story, and the evangelists make no attempt to create such stories on their own. Still, in view of the paucity of evidence one way or the other, I can readily understand why some scholars may prefer a judgement of *non liquet* or even Rochais' judgement of historical. Nevertheless, given the anchoring of Luke 7:11-17 in the otherwise unheard-of town of Nain plus this general tendency of the traditions of the Four Gospels, I incline (with some hesitation) to the view that the story goes back to some incident involving Jesus at Nain during his public ministry'. *A Marginal Jew – Rethinking the historical Jesus: Volume Two – Mentor, Message and Miracles* (New York: Doubleday, 1994), 797-798

Jesus' reaching out to human beings, his compassion drawn by nothing else save their state of affliction'.[158]

The Master of Mercy

The story of the healing of the ten lepers (17:11-19)[159] is found only in *Luke* 'and represents an expansion of the cleansing of the leper in 5:12-16'.[160] There 'a man covered with leprosy' meets Jesus and bowing before him begs, 'Lord, if you choose, you can make me clean'. Jesus' immediate response is to reach out and touch him, telling the leper in emotive terms 'I do choose. Be made clean'. This encounter resembles the story of the raising of the widow's son with the exception that the leper asks Jesus to heal him. Replying to this request in the exact terms in which it is made Jesus exhibits a deep desire to restore the leper to health and reintegrate him into the community. Luke omits the matter of Jesus' motivation as mentioned by Mark, that is, he was 'moved with pity' (1:41).[161] The later (and longer) story of the healing of the ten lepers involves a shift of scene from 'one of the cities' to the countryside. By beginning his account with a reference to Jesus' continuing journey to Jerusalem the evangelist is not simply stating a geographical detail in the story but showing the significance of Jesus' destination and his

---

[158]   *The Hospitality of God*, 70

[159]   For a discussion of the issues involved in the interpretation of these miracle stories see Meier, 'Persons Afflicted with "Leprosy"', ibid 698-700

[160]   Johnson, *The Gospel of Luke*, 261

[161]   Also Matthew does not mention the motivation of Jesus in his version of the healing miracle. For a discussion of the textual tradition and translation(s) see Robert H. Stein, *Mark* (Grand Rapids: Michigan, 2008), 110-111.

denouement there. The passage of the prophet 'through the region between Samaria and Galilee' has powerful portents for the identity of the Church and inclusion within it.

After describing the movement(s) of Jesus – 'on the way to Jerusalem...he entered a village' – Luke paints the plight of the ten lepers with pathos. They approach Jesus while at the same time 'keeping their distance'. Though not hesitating to ask for help they hold back. With the exposition of their request and reticence the evangelist evokes pity for them. Unlike the narrative at Nain the ten take the initiative by approaching Jesus, calling on him by name: 'Jesus, Master, have mercy on us'. After seeing them – like he saw the widow – Jesus simply commands them to go and show themselves to the priests. The absence of any reference to his motivation on this occasion is perhaps explained by the evangelist's estimation that it is unnecessary or that it is partially expressed in their call for mercy. As they head off, healed, one of them turns back and, praising God, prostrates himself before Jesus and thanks him. Jesus asks rhetorically about the 'ten made clean' and as to where the other nine are. Having already alerted readers to the identity of the one who returned (a Samaritan) Luke has Jesus refer to the fact that he is a 'foreigner' whose 'faith has made [him] well' (17:19). Boivon remarks that 'Luke used that addition to call attention to the fact that God's mercy in Jesus Christ has broken religious barriers and called into question any and every particularistic definition of Israel's election'.[162]

---

[162] *Luke 2 (A Commentary on the Gospel of Luke 9:51-19:27)*, (Minneapolis: Fortress Press, 2013), 505

The recognition of Jesus as 'Master' by the ten – the only occasion that this is done by those who are not disciples – reinforces not only the dependency but also the devotion due to him. Thus Mary Healy states:

The New Testament frequently refers to Jesus' healings, together with exorcisms and other miraculous works, as 'signs and wonders'. This phrase signifies two related dimensions. First, healings are 'signs' because they are a revelation of Jesus' divine identity and messianic mission. They visibly manifest his love and compassion for suffering humanity and his definitive victory over sin and death. Second, healings are 'wonders' because they elicit a response of awe, wonder, praise and gratitude. It is clear, however, that physical healings are not an end in themselves; the account of the ten lepers…for example, suggest[s] that healing is only complete when it has drawn the recipient into a relationship with Jesus in which he is recognized and worshipped for who he is'.[163]

The Messiah of Mercy

Listing another landmark – 'as he approached Jericho' - on Jesus' journey to Jerusalem, Luke tells the story of the healing of the blind beggar (18:35-43). Hearing the noise of 'a crowd going by, he asked what was happening' and when given the answer that 'Jesus of Nazareth is passing by', immediately implores the Nazerene thus: 'Jesus, Son of David, have mercy on me'. Instructed by those at the front of the crowd to be

---

[163] 'A Catholic Perspective on Healing', *One In Christ*, 47 (2013), 285-310, here 289

quiet he ignores their stern injunction and raises his voice to beg again, 'Son of David, have mercy on me'. The response of Jesus is immediate, stopping in his tracks and saying that the man should be brought to him, inquiring directly, 'What do you want me to do for you?' Acceding to the blind man's request, Jesus replies 'Receive your sight', adding that his faith has saved him. Having recovered his sight instantaneously, he follows Jesus 'glorifying God'. The evangelist embellishes the effect of the individual's encounter with Jesus by expressing that when 'all the people saw it' they too 'praised God'.

A feature common to many of the miracles of Jesus is illustrated in these three stories, that is, their immediacy.[164] The story of the blind man being restored to sight combines elements of the two miracles, at Nain and in the unnamed village.

Like the ten lepers, the blind man lives up to his identity by begging Jesus to heal him. As with the one leper who returned to render thanks Jesus commends the faith of the blind man. Like the people who witnessed the raising of the widow's son, the crowd who saw the blind man receiving his sight back join in praising God for what Jesus has done. This confession celebrates that these miracles are caused by the power of God which Jesus proclaimed and made present. The call for mercy

---

[164] 'There is never an account of a long procedure like those characteristic of many medicine women and men, shamans, and healers. We must assume that the miracle stories in the gospels depict many things in summary and are condensations of more complex events. Nevertheless, the "immediacy" of most of these narratives is apparent. The eyewitnesses were moved and shaken by Jesus' power and authority'. Gerhard Lohfink, 'How Did Jesus Heal?', in *No Irrelevant Jesus* (Collegeville, MN: Michael Glazier, 2014), 62

uttered by both the lepers and the beggar is made with the same word – *eleos* – used in both the *Magnificat* and *Benedictus*. The manifestation of mercy in and through the miracles of Jesus means that the promise of God's visitation made before his birth has now come to pass. This incarnate mercy inhabits places like Nain and Jericho where Jesus encounters human need for healing from illness and delivery from death. Contrasting this mercy with magic Lohfink points out the crucial difference: 'Jesus' healings occur within a different realm of meaning, namely, the context of the reign of God'.[165] Ultimately this raises the question of Jesus' own identity, that is, his relationship to the God he calls his heavenly Father.

---

[165]   Ibid, 58

Chapter Five

Parables of Pity

'Jesus' parables are among the best known and most influential stories in the world. Even if people know nothing of Jesus, they either know about his stories or have encountered their impact in expressions like "prodigal" or "good Samaritan". The importance of the parables of Jesus can hardly be overestimated'.[166]

Preaching in Parables

'He began to teach them many things in parables' (Mk 4:2). While Luke does not follow Mark in this summary statement of the style and substance of Jesus' proclamation (unlike Matthew, though not verbatim, 'And he told them many things in parables', 13:3), parables play a prominent part of his presentation of Jesus' message, the proclamation of the Kingdom of God. The parables of Jesus are not self-referential but revelatory. They represent his style and manner of relating to people. Gerald O' Collins and Daniel Kendall capture well Jesus' way with words in welcoming people:

'No matter what one's faith, Jesus' power of language entitles him to be ranked as one of history's most extraordinary communicators. He spoke with

---

[166]   *Stories with Intent – A Comprehensive Guide to the Parables of Jesus*, 1.

authority and at times in a remarkably innovative way. Nevertheless, he never employed linguistic skills to dominate or manipulate his audiences. The parables called on people to respond freely to the divine presence that was powerfully at work to heal and transform their lives. Jesus never used his powers of communication to demand submission, but rather invited others to identify with him in sharing a vision of the Father who offers an unconditional love to all persons'.[167]

A parable is not a logical proposition but a theological word picture and therefore, in the words of Jacques Dupont, 'cannot have meaning apart from its relation to a *something beyond*'.[168] For Klyne R. Snodgrass 'parables were the means Jesus used most frequently to explain the kingdom of God and the expectations God has for humans'.[169] This 'communicative intent of Jesus'[170] inherent in the parables involves the four 'I's important for Luke, viz. invitation and inclusion, integrity and implementation. In keeping with the theme of divine hospitality, the Lucan Jesus issues invitation after invitation to individuals to inherit the kingdom he proclaims and makes present. The parable of the *Great Dinner* comes after the saying about not inviting 'your friends or your brothers or your relatives or rich neighbours, in case they may invite you in return' (14:13). When the many initially invited to the dinner decline this is extended

---

[167] 'Jesus the Communicator' in *Focus on Jesus*, (Hertfordshire: Gracewing, 1996), 64-65.

[168] Quoted in Bosetti, *Luke – The Song of God's Mercy*, k101

[169] *Stories with Intent*, 2

[170] Ibid

to 'the poor, the crippled, the blind, and the lame' and those out on 'the roads and lanes' (14:21, 23), an offer which shows both the option and openness that are obviously important to the evangelist.

Inclusion is clearly intended and indicated in Luke's three parables of the lost – sheep, coin and son(s). Jesus' rhetorical question gives the lie to the grumbling Pharisees and scribes – 'Which one of you... does not leave the ninety-nine in the wilderness and go after the one that is lost until he finds it?' (15:4). No mention is made of the risk of losing any of the ninety-nine in this search-and rescue mission. Luke's insistence on moral character and integrity is a key issue in the parables of the widow and unjust judge (18:1-8) and the ten pounds (19:11-27). The lack of integrity of the judge 'who neither feared God nor had respect for people' (18:2) means that he will only do the work of justice because the widow is wearing him out by her 'continually coming' (18:5). The man who wrapped up the pound entrusted to him denies the nobleman the possibility of gaining on his investment while the others trade with their pounds and acquire a twofold profit, thus earning trustworthiness and taking charge of cities rather than coins. Implementation is integral to Jesus' instruction in the parables, as the ending of the *Good Samaritan* indicates – 'Go and do likewise' (10:37). Snodgrass states this performative feature firmly:

> Some parables are as clear as bells, and, while we may discuss nuances and backgrounds in lengthy treatises, they do not need explanation so much as implementation.

They in effect say to us, "Stop resisting and do it", or "Believe it". We do not need much commentary to know the intent of the parable of the Good Samaritan. Despite the numerous studies of this parable... the parable compels us to stop resisting and live it.[171]

Snodgrass' reference to 'studies' raises the issue of interpretation, noting that 'a history of interpretation is virtually a prerequisite for studying Jesus' parables'.[172] A particular instance is what Snodgrass calls 'allegorizing', a practice he illustrates with 'Augustine's interpretation of the parable of the Good Samaritan, in which virtually every item is given theological significance'.[173] This methodological approach is akin to the proof-text attribution of scriptural quotes in the pre-conciliar manuals of moral theology. Itemizing the parts of parables incurs the proverbial danger of missing the wood for the trees and mistaking a detail for what is decisive. After describing the meaning of the Greek word *parabol* as used in the Gospels and delineating six categories for classifying the parables,[174] Snodgrass sets out a long list of the characteristics of the parables of Jesus.[175] Brief and anonymous (except for Lazarus and Abraham in Lk 16:19-31), they are simple in

---

[171] Ibid, 3
[172] Ibid. For an overview of the history of what he calls 'Parable Exegesis' up to 1990 see J.R Donahue, 'The Parables of Jesus', in eds R.E. Brown, J.A. Fitzmyer, R.E. Murphy, *The New Jerome Biblical Commentary* (Englewood Cliffs, New Jersey: Prentice Hall, 1990), pars. 61-71, 1365-1366. See also John Dominic Crossan, 'The Parables of Jesus', *Interpretation*, 56 (July 2002): 247-259
[173] *Stories with Intent – A Comprehensive Guide to the Parables of Jesus*, 4
[174] *Stories with Intent*, 10-15
[175] Ibid, 17- 22

focus and symmetrical in function. Drawing from everyday examples of human experience they are engaging, 'used to draw hearers in and compel dealing with the issues at hand'.[176] Often interrogative in form, 'finding the implied question a parable addresses is key in interpretation'.[177] The parables are particular and placed in a context, drawing out a specific point and not deducing from general moral principles. Working within the hermeneutical horizon of heralding the reign of God the parables are products of Jesus' incarnate imagination. As prophetic statements they pronounce in sayings, similes or stories the presence of God's Kingdom among their hearers. In addition to announcing they also ask for – and in case(s) of denouncing they demand – change from current patterns of relating and behaving. Featuring reversal in many instances, the parables 'are among the most powerful instruments for change that Jesus used'.[178] Barbara E. Reid comments on this central characteristic of Jesus' parabolic preaching:

> There is usually an unexpected twist: a hated Samaritan takes care of a wounded Jew after a priest and a Levite pass him by (Lk 10:25-37); a humble toll collector's prayer shows him to be more justified than a pious Pharisee (Luke 18:9-14); a persistent widow reflects God's passion for right relations rather than a judge entrusted with upholding justice (Lk 18:1-8). The twist disrupts one's expectations. Like a boomerang, the unexpected turn can make the parable swing back at the

---

[176]   Ibid, 18
[177]   Ibid, 19
[178]   Ibid

hearers, confronting them with the need to change their attitude or behaviour… Parables are not nice stories that confirm the *status quo*. They are disturbing and puzzling and usually invite conversion.[179]

Thus the parables play a central part in Jesus' proclamation and the moral-spiritual conversion it proposes to people. Challenging the conscience of their audience(s) to consider their way of living, the parables 'seek to goad people into the action the gospel deserves'.[180] While frequently presented in bundles the parables are particular and 'each one must be analysed in its own right to determine how it functions'.[181] The functioning of individual parables must be interpreted in terms of the theological interest(s) of each evangelist. The redactional involvement of the individual Synoptics in placing and presenting particular parables is a reminder that 'the parables are stories used twice – once by Jesus and then again by the Evangelists'.[182] As stories a very significant principle of their interpretation is the 'rule of end stress' which insists that 'for most parables what comes at the end is the clinching indicator of intent'[183]. The theological import – and therefore importance – of the parables is stressed by Snodgrass:

> The parables of Jesus do not reveal the whole of Christian theology by any means. Without the cross

---

[179] 'Jesus: Parabolic Preacher', *The Bible Today*, 52 (2014), 207-21, here 209

[180] *Stories with Intent*, 9

[181] Ibid, 22

[182] Ibid. Snodgrass notes that 'in the technical sense there are no parables in John'

[183] Ibid, 30

and resurrection Christian theology would not exist. However, the parables provide material for a compelling and convincing picture of Jesus' teaching on the kingdom, his understanding of God, and the kind of life expected of his disciples, whether they live in the first or the twenty-first century. The theology of these stories merits our investment in them.[184]

Parables for Pilgrims

Luke's investment in the parables of Jesus is indicated by the fact that together they make up more than half of his *Gospel*.[185] The central section of *Luke* (9:51-19:27) is framed around the narrative of Jesus' journey to Jerusalem. This orientation is obvious from the outset: 'When the days drew near for him to be taken up, he set his face to go to Jerusalem' (9:51). Jesus does not undertake this journey alone but is accompanied by his disciples and anyone who would accept to identify with the bold assertion of an anonymous man they meet on the way, 'I will follow you wherever you go' (9:57). For Luke this account is not a travelogue but teaching, an itinerary with inbuilt instruction; as Jean-Noël Aletti states: 'Jesus effectively seizes the occasion of the journey to form his disciples, not only in telling them how they should address God and act with others but also in revealing to them the mysteries of the Kingdom'.[186] The many parables placed in this part of *Luke* and especially those that are particular to the evangelist play

---

184   Ibid, 31
185   Ibid, 22
186   *Le Jésus De Luc* (Paris: MamE-Desclée, 2010), 129. (My Translation)

a prominent part in this process. These words of Jesus on the way to Jerusalem are both formative and normative for the way of Christian discipleship.

Mikeal C. Parsons lists twenty-five parables in the 'Lucan Travel Narrative', of which ten are attributable as specific to *Luke*.[187] Gerard S. Sloyan's comment credits the genius of Luke in grafting these ten parables onto the narrative: 'The parables of Jesus proper to Luke are more helpful to discover the skill of the Master as teacher than would be the small ways in which he edited the material he got from Mark or had in common with Matthew'.[188] Following Donahue's lead that 'the parables reflect distinct Lucan themes and theology… and "compassion" is important in Luke's parables'[189], the focus falls on four of the ten that are found only in *Luke*. These are the *Good Samaritan* (10: 29-37), the *Lost Son and Brother* (15:11-32), the *Rich Man and Lazarus* (16:19-31) and the *Pharisee and Tax Collector* (18: 9-14). These represent the 'special Lucan parables of the lengthy "tale" type, which teach by narration of a particular incident rather than by analogy'.[190] Taken together these parables of pity proclaim what might be termed 'The Gospel of Mercy according to Luke'. Interestingly, in his exposition of the parables of Jesus Pope Benedict XVI/Joseph Ratzinger limits himself to treating the first three of these, referring to 'the three major parable narratives

---

[187] *Luke – Storyteller, Interpreter, Evangelist* (Peabody, Mass: Hendrickson Publishers, 2007), 116-117

[188] *Jesus – Word Made Flesh* (Collegeville, MN: Liturgical Press, 2008), 93

[189] 'The Parables of Jesus', 1368. Joseph A. Fitzmyer speaks of 'the great Lucan parables of mercy', *The Gospel According to LUKE (X-XXIV)*, (New York: Doubleday & Company, Inc, 1985), 1184.

[190] C. F. Evans, *Saint Luke*, (London: SCM Press, 1990), 467

in Luke's Gospel, whose beauty and depth spontaneously touch believer and nonbeliever alike again and again'.[191]

The Parable of the Compassionate Samaritan[192]

The parable popularly known as the *Good Samaritan*[193] is placed in the first chapter of the 'Lukan Travel Narrative' and, as David Lyle Jeffrey declares, 'in Luke's schema for his Gospel, it comes near to the midpoint of his symmetrically organized narrative and is in the spiritual sense a synecdoche, a précis of the whole biblical story of salvation'.[194] The parable forms the conclusion of a conversation begun by a lawyer who 'stood up to test Jesus' (10:25). He did this by asking about what he should 'do to inherit eternal life' (10:25). The dynamic of the exchange is developed by Luke to show that Jesus is effectively in control of the encounter, despite the obvious grandstanding of the lawyer. Jesus' commendation of his correct answer combining the commandments of love of God and 'neighbour as himself' does not end the matter. Attributing the motive of 'wanting to justify himself' (10:29), Luke lets the lawyer interrogate Jesus further by inquiring about the identity of the neighbour. This leads to the parable which begins with an anonymous figure travelling away from Jerusalem just as Jesus is heading there. The victim of a vicious assault, he is left 'half dead'. A priest and

[191] *Jesus of Nazareth*, (London: Bloomsbury, 2007), 194
[192] This is the title given by both C. F. Evans in *Saint Luke*, 466 and Joel B. Green in *The Gospel of Luke*, 424
[193] 'This parable of the Good Samaritan is one of the most well known parables in the New Testament and one of the most quoted stories from all world literature'. Mullins, *The Gospel of Luke,* 310
[194] *Luke*, 151

Levite are described as travelling on the same road and seeing him though they do nothing for him, both opting to pass by 'on the other side'. Employing the phrase 'saw him' for a third time, the evangelist introduces a Samaritan who is 'moved with pity' for the wounded man. Pope Benedict XVI states how the Gospel brings out the Samaritan's gut reaction:

> His heart is wrenched open. The Gospel uses the word that in Hebrew had originally referred to the mother's womb and maternal care. Seeing this man in such a state is a blow that strikes him "viscerally", touching his soul. "He had compassion" – that is how we translate the text today, diminishing its original vitality. Struck in his soul by the lightning flash of mercy, he himself now becomes a neighbour, heedless of any question or danger.[195]

After administering first aid the Samaritan carries him to an inn and pays the innkeeper to continue caring for him, pledging to come back and reimburse any further expense incurred. Turning the terms of the lawyer's question around Jesus asks him about the identity of the one who proved to be a neighbour to the man in need. After receiving the obvious answer – 'The one who showed him mercy' – Jesus ends by exhorting the lawyer to copy his example – 'Go and do likewise' (10:37). As Judith Schubert states, 'this provocative remark commands the lawyer to follow in the footsteps of his enemy… to let go of his smugness, to open his heart and transcend the boundaries of his limited view of "neighbour", and to act as a "neighbour" to anyone in need'.[196]

---

[195] *Jesus of Nazareth*, 197
[196] 'The Parable of the Good Samaritan – *A Compassionate Enemy*', *The Bible Today*, 45 (January 2007):22-26, here 26

Reference to 'when he [the Samaritan] saw him, he was moved with pity' (10:33) not only recalls but repeats Jesus' (earlier) response to the widow at Nain: 'When the Lord saw her, he had compassion for her' (7:13). Luke employs the same verb to express the source and strength of the mercy shown by both Jesus towards the widow who has lost her son and the Samaritan towards the man who has nearly lost his life. While the *NRSV* translates these differently - 'compassion' in the case of Jesus and 'pity' in the case of the Samaritan – the meaning is the same as both are motivated by mercy and moved to help. While Jesus and the Samaritan differ in their capacity to respond, viz. raising the dead young man at Nain to life and restoring the wounded man to health, the concatenation of their concern is the chief link between both miracle and parable. The continuity between the compassion of Jesus and that of the Samaritan is clearly commended by the evangelist to communicate that compassion is central to both the mission and message of Jesus. Similarly Luke employs Zechariah's words 'he has shown the mercy' – *eleos* – to express continuity between the covenantal love of God for humanity and the contribution the Samaritan makes to the welfare of the wounded man. Amy-Jill Levine draws out and dovetails the incarnational implication and imperative of this parable of pity:

> The parable spoke about compassion, but the lawyer read the action as one of mercy. His rephrasing the issue is apt: compassion can be felt in the gut; mercy needs to be enacted with the body. The term may come from Luke, who uses it extensively, but only in the infancy

materials, where mercy is an attribute of the divine: For the lawyer, and for Luke's readers, the Samaritan does what God does. The divine is manifested only through our actions. Therefore, Jesus responds to the lawyer's observation not with a question and not with a parable, but with an imperative: "Go", he says, "and you do likewise".[197]

There are two reversals in the story and they are related, revealing two sides of the same coin. Firstly introducing the identity of the one who gave succour to the wounded man as a Samaritan is an interruption that is surprising, to say the least. As *The Jewish Annotated New Testament* (NRSV) asserts, 'the parable shocks by making the third person not the expected Israelite but the unexpected Samaritan, the enemy of the Jews'.[198] Secondly, in reframing the lawyer's question the response of Jesus rolls the responsibility back onto him (and all hearers), effectively asking him not 'who is my neighbour' but 'who am I willing to be neighbour to'.[199] As Sabourin states, 'at the beginning the "neighbour" is the person helped, at the end it is every person who through compassion comes to the aid of people in need'.[200] Neil Brown states: 'here, being "neighbour" crosses all social, religious and racial boundaries to be expressed

---

[197] 'Go and Do Likewise – Lessons from the Parable of the Good Samaritan', *America* (29 September 2014):16-18, here 18

[198] Eds, Amy-Jill Levine and Marc Zvi Brettler (Oxford: Oxford University Press, 2011), 123

[199] See Michael Fagenblat, 'The Concept of Neighbour in Jewish and Christian Ethics', in *The Jewish Annotated New Testament*, 540-543

[200] *L'Évangile de Luc*, 225 (My translation)

in compassion and effective aid to any person in need'.[201] Thus, it is a matter, in Mullins' words, of being 'neighbour to the other, especially to the other who is in need, irrespective of who that person happens to be'.[202] Mercy merges compassion as the capacity to recognize others as one's neighbour with pity that is prepared to relate properly and practically to them.[203]

Joseph A. Fitzmyer indicates that 'the incorporation of this episode into this Gospel emphasizes that part of the *Sermon on the Plain* that deals with human love (6:27-35)'.[204] Appeals to the parable are often cast in terms of combining biblical *agape/love* and ethical altruism as a basis for action. Considered as a story of moral exemplarism *par excellence* the parable of the 'Good Samaritan' is often featured as an encouragement to enact the Golden Rule. Judith Schubert expounds:

This unique and boundary-breaking parable reflects the theology of the Gospel of Luke: it represents ideas about who God is and how God encourages and empowers us to behave. It emerges as a key example of Jesus' instructions about the need for mercy, inclusiveness, compassion, forgiveness, repentance, and love of neighbour, especially the marginalized.[205]

---

[201] 'The Dynamism of Charity in the Moral Life', *The Australasian Catholic Record*, 80 (2003), 451-465, here 453

[202] *The Gospel of Luke*, 312

[203] See Donal Murray, 'Towards a Real Discovery of the Other' in ed Eoin G. Cassidy, *Who Is My Neighbour?* (Dublin: Veritas, 2009), 56-77

[204] *The Gospel According to Luke (X-XXIV)*, 884

[205] 'The Parable of the Good Samaritan', *The Bible Today*, 45 (2007): 22-27, here 23

An illustration of this, sadly one of inversion, is a hit-and-run incident in China involving a two-year-old girl. Reporting — ironically reported on the feast of Saint Luke – Clifford Coonan relates how

> 'the harrowing footage, broadcast on Southern Television Guangdong, shows how nearly 20 pedestrians and passing vehicles kept going without coming to the child's aid. One young man walks past, apparently without seeing her, but others pass and look down, doing nothing. A mother hurries her daughter away from the scene.[206]

Reporting on reaction to the story in the country Michael Sheridan noted that criticism of callousness on the part of those who passed by was countered by 'many people [who] pointed to highly publicized court cases against Good Samaritans who had helped accident victims, only to find themselves blamed and forced to pay for medical bills'.[207] Snodgrass' statement that the parable of the compassionate Samaritan 'has been applied to virtually every aspect of ethics'[208] is important because it indicates the fundamental relationship between mercy and morality, not least in relation to religious ethics.

---

[206] 'Outrage over passersby ignoring dying child in China', *The Irish Times*, 18 October 2011

[207] 'It's cheaper to kill, say China hit-and-runs', *The Sunday Times*, 23 October 2011

[208] *Stories with Intent*, 360. For a discussion of ethical theories, especially virtue ethics and the parable see Samuel K. Roberts, 'Becoming the Neighbour: Virtue Theory and the Problem of Neighbour Identity', *Interpretation*, 62 (2008):146-155

In his encyclical *Deus Caritas Est (God is Love)*, Pope Benedict XVI points out how Luke, in the parable of the compassionate Samaritan, underscores two vital implications of the Gospel message and mission of Jesus, universalism and undertaking:

> Until that time, the concept of "neighbour" was understood as referring essentially to one's countrymen and to foreigners who had settled in the land of Israel; in other words, to the closely-knit community of a single country or people. This limit is now abolished. Anyone who needs me, and whom I can help, is my neighbour. The concept of "neighbour" is now universalized, yet it remains concrete. Despite being extended to all humankind, it is not reduced to a generic, abstract and undemanding expression of love, but calls for my own practical commitment here and now. The Church has the duty to interpret ever anew this relationship between near and far with regard to the actual daily life of her members.[209]

The urgency of universalizing respect for all people, recognizing their rights and responding to their needs is a critical characteristic of contemporary moral consciousness. Globalization must not only be economic but ethical. Increasing international tension(s) and regional conflicts, sometimes with religious overtones, calls for a continual reminder and restatement of the story of the Samaritan with its ethic of

---

[209]   (Vatican City: *Libreria Editrice Vaticana*, 2006), 15

universalism united with an undertaking to imitate his showing of mercy to the stranger in need. At the same time Benedict gives the lie to any general ethic which eschews engagement with the local and particular. His reference to 'near and far' both guides and grounds what Michael P. Hornsby-Smith calls 'a globalization of compassion'[210], thus echoing his predecessor's plea for interdependent solidarity which 'is not a feeling of vague compassion or shallow distress at the misfortunes of so many people, both near and far' but a commitment to 'the common good; that is to say to the good of all and of each individual, because we are all really responsible for all'.[211]

Pope Francis offers an imaginative insight into the parable, interpreting 'neighbourliness' in terms of communication through contemporary technology:

How can we be "neighbourly" in our use of the communications media and the new environment created by digital technology? I find an answer in the parable of the Good Samaritan, which is also a parable about communication. Those who communicate, in effect, become neighbours... Jesus shifts our understanding: it is not just about seeing the other as someone like myself, but of the ability to make myself like the other. Communication is really about realizing that we are all human beings, children of God. I like seeing this power of com-

[210] *An Introduction to Catholic Social Thought*, (Cambridge: Cambridge University Press, 2006), 4.
[211] Pope John Paul II, *Sollicitudo Rei Socialis* (1987), 38 (http://w2.vatican.va/content/john-paul-ii/en/encyclicals/documents/papa-jp-ii) [accessed 25/09/2014]

munication as "neighbourliness"...It is not enough to be passersby on the digital highways, simply "connected"; connections need to grow into true encounters... Christian witness, thanks to the internet, can thereby reach the peripheries of human existence.[212]

Combining Francis' evangelical emphasis on 'encounter' with his missionary concern for people on 'the peripheries of human existence', the *Good/Compassionate Samaritan* is hereby presented as a parable for our times. With its almost infinite possibilities for exchange and empathy between people, the internet and social media offer and open up previously unimagined avenues to answer the question 'Who is my neighbour?'.

The Parable of the Compassionate Parent

François Bovon notes that Luke uses the singular 'this parable' (15:3) to signify three – the lost sheep, the lost coin, the lost son – and refers to them as 'the parables of mercy'.[213] Traditionally termed *The Parable of the Prodigal Son*, the third parable (15:11-32) has in recent times been broadened to include reference to his brother as, for example, *The Parable of the Prodigal and his Brother*, in the version of *The Gospel of Luke* distributed jointly by Church of Ireland United Dioceses of Dublin & Glendalough and the Catholic Archdiocese of Dublin

---

[212] 'Communication at the Service of an Authentic Culture of Encounter', *Message for the 48th World Communications Day*, (http://w2.vatican.va/content/francesco/en/messages/communications/documents/papa-frances) [accessed 13/06/2014].

[213] *Luke 2*, 399-400

for *The Year of Evangelization*.[214] This tendency to increasingly involve the two siblings in the story also reflects the practice of preaching with an allegorical application of the sons as standing for different attitudes towards the law and life. However, the figure of the father looms large, featuring from the first line – 'Then Jesus said, "There was a man who had two sons"(15:11) – 'and forming a link with the final line where he pleads with the elder son to enter into the spirit of the party put on to welcome the wayward son back 'because this brother of yours was dead and has come to life' (15:32). Like the sheep and the coin in the previous two parables he too 'was lost and has been found' (15:32). Often a figure of pity himself in homilies based on this Gospel because of what he had to put up with from his children, the father is the hero of the hour as he personifies the archetypal father figure. Dedicated to his own father, Henri Nouwen declared that his well known book *The Return of the Prodigal Son* (inspired by the painting of the same name held in The Hermitage, Saint Petersburg) 'could easily have been called "The Welcome by the Compassionate Father" [as] the emphasis is less on the son than on the father... [and] looking at the way in which Rembrandt portrays the father, there came to me a whole new interior understanding of tenderness, mercy and forgiveness'.[215]

The father gives both freedom and fortune to the younger son when he asks. Ending up in a faraway country he finds himself in dire straits, reduced to feeding pigs and not earning

---

[214] (Dublin: Veritas, 2010), 44
[215] (London: Darton, Longman and Todd Ltd, 1994), 92-93

enough to even eat what they receive. Coming to his senses, he realizes that many of his 'father's hired hands have bread enough and to spare' and 'dying of hunger' (15:13) he decides to head home. Having prepared and recited his confession many times on the journey back he finds his father coming towards him and throwing his arms around him tenderly. The feeling of not being 'worthy to be called your son' falls away from the scene as quickly as he is welcomed and wrapped with 'a robe –the best one' (15:22). His homecoming is celebrated with a banquet. The father's older son returns from working in the field and receives the news of his brother's reception with resentment, refusing to join in the festivities. Coming out to him the father 'began to plead with him', only to be lectured about his own lifelong obedience and berated about bringing out 'the fatted calf' for 'this son of yours who has devoured your property with prostitutes' (15:30). In response the father repeats the reason for rejoicing, replacing 'this son of mine' (15:24) with 'this brother of yours' who 'was dead and has come to life; he was lost and has been found' (15:32).

The parable plays out like a three-act drama dominated by movement, metaphorical as well as literal. In the first the younger son asks his father for 'the share of the property that will belong to me' (15:12) and goes away to squander his inheritance. The nadir of his alienation is neatly (no irony intended!) in the sight of him feeding pigs, 'a terribly shameful state for a Jew to find himself slave of an unclean Gentile and worse still looking after the animals the Jews regarded as unclean'.[216] Remembering

---

[216] Mullins, *The Gospel of Luke*, 362

his father's household he realizes that he would be immensely better off at home and returns there in a state of repentance. The second act shows the father scanning the horizon, hoping that his prodigal son will appear. At the first sighting the father runs to meet him with a kiss, the gesture of greeting that recognizes 'him as son even before the child has a chance to state his repentance'.[217] The subsequent celebration sets the scene for the third act. Here the older brother stops short of joining the party on hearing from one of the 'hired hands' that 'your brother has come, and your father has killed the fatted calf, because he has got him back safe and sound' (15:27), a remark that drives him into a rage, ranting about the relative merits of his own duty and daily work in contrast with the dissipation and dedicated waste of his younger sibling. The parable/play finishes with the father going out from the joyful gathering to assure him that 'you are always with me, and all that is mine is yours' (15:31) and asking him to show some of the same magnanimity. Rather than ordering his older son the father invites him to imitate the compassionate Samaritan – 'Go and do likewise'. In this case the intended recipient is not a stranger but a sibling.

After pointing out that patristic commentators 'put all their love into their exposition' of the scene of the son's embrace by the father, seeing the son as a symbol of fallen humanity, Joseph Ratzinger – now Pope Emeritus Benedict XVI – states that 'the kernel of the text is unmistakably the figure of the father'.[218] In describing the father's response to his returning and admittedly

[217]   Johnson, *The Gospel of Luke*, 241
[218]   *Jesus of Nazareth*, 206

repentant younger son – 'filled with compassion' (15:20) – Luke again uses the same verb as before to show that this emanates from the depths of the father's being. Snodgrass states that this expression of 'the eagerness of the father to recover and restore the erring son is poignantly and tenderly described'.[219] The father's compassion for his son is the same as that sensed and shown by both Jesus for the widow at Nain (7:13) and the Samaritan for the wounded man by the wayside (10:33). The effects of these encounters and expressions of mercy are equivalent. As Jesus raised the young man from the dead and 'gave him to his mother' (7:15), so too the Samaritan saves the man from death while the father receives his younger child as someone returned from the dead, 'for this son of mine was dead and is alive again' (15:24). Mercy both moves the principal actors – Jesus, the Samaritan, the father – in these stories and makes a life of meaning – in mortal, medicinal and moral terms respectively – for their recipients.

In each of the three 'parables of mercy' in Luke 15 there is an element of excess which could lead to economic ruin. The shepherd leaves the ninety nine to go in search of the single stray sheep. Notwithstanding elements of danger in the search and rescue mission, he runs the risk of losing many more to either attack by wild animals or robbery by unscrupulous shepherds. Common sense would seem to dictate cutting one's loss and letting the balance sheet show the benefit of a strategy of prudence. The process of losing and finding the lost coin costs the woman a lot, possibly even more than its value as

---

[219] *Stories with Intent*, 140

she spends so much on throwing a party. The father allows his younger son to gather his share and go his own way, not asking for any accountability when he returns home penniless. The focal point of the parable is the father's attitude. If he had interrogated the younger son on his return, insisting on an inventory of his act of squandering his inheritance, a very different image would have emerged. Instead the adjective 'prodigal' applies to the father's mercy rather than to the son's mess. As Aletti asserts, 'in reality, the father described by the parable represents *God the Father and him alone*, who rejoices at the return of sinners, who, by forgiveness above all, tries to make them enter into his merciful design'.[220] Joseph Fitzmyer fully supports this interpretation: 'As it now stands in the Lucan Gospel, the parable presents the loving father as a symbol of God Himself. His ready, unconditioned, and unstinted love and mercy are manifested not only towards the repentant sinner (the younger son) but towards the uncomprehending critic of such a human being'.[221]

Léopold Sabourin links the parables in *Luke 15* under the label 'Three parables on the divine mercy'.[222] The disclosure of this mercy is designed to answer the complaint of the scribes and Pharisees about Jesus, 'This fellow welcomes sinners and eats with them' (15:2). As the prophet of God's pity Jesus proclaims the message of divine mercy in these parables of searching and

---

[220]   *Le Jésus De Luc,* 153 (My translation)

[221]   *The Gospel According to Luke (X-XXIV),* New York: Doubleday & Company, 1985, 1085

[222]   *L'Évangile De Luc – Introduction et Commentaire,* Rome: Editrice Pontificia Universitá Gregoriana, 1987, 273 (My translation)

welcoming where love reaches out to recover and restore the lost. As well as silencing his critics Jesus communicates to his disciples a sense of the compassion that lies at the heart of the household of God. Robert J. Karris comments on this Gospel thread that runs through these parables:

> In three parables Luke champions the theme that God's mercy breaks through all human restrictions of how God should act towards sinners. God's mercy, indeed, is as foolish as a shepherd who abandons 99 sheep to save a stray one, as a woman who turns her house upside down to recover a paltry sum, and as a Jewish father who joyfully welcomes home his wastrel son who has become a Gentile. Because disciples have such a merciful God, they can embark trustingly and joyfully on Jesus' way to God.[223]

In his second encyclical *Dives in misericordia* (*Rich in mercy*), Pope John Paul II begins by referring to 'The Revelation of Mercy: It is "God, who is rich in mercy" [Eph 2:4] whom Jesus Christ has revealed to us as Father'.[224] After treating of the 'Incarnation of mercy' or the 'Messianic Message' and the theme of mercy in the Old Testament he turns to the 'Parable of the Prodigal Son'. After acknowledging that 'at the very beginning of the New Testament, two voices [Mary and Zechariah] resound in St Luke's Gospel in unique harmony concerning the mercy of God, a harmony which forcefully echoes the whole Old

---

[223] *The Gospel According To Luke*, in *The New Jerome Biblical Commentary*, 707

[224] http://w2.vatican.va/content/john-paul-ii/en/encyclicals/documents/hf_jp-ii_enc_3011_dives-in-misericordia, 1 [accessed 24/09/2014]

Testament tradition' while 'the word "mercy" does not appear' in the parable 'it nevertheless expresses the essence of the divine mercy in a particularly clear way'. [225] The Pope's interpretation of the parable is analogical rather than allegorical:

> There is no doubt that in this simple but penetrating analogy the figure of the father reveals to us God as Father. The conduct of the father in the parable and his whole behaviour, which manifests his internal attitude, enables us to rediscover the individual threads of the Old Testament vision of mercy in a synthesis which is totally new, full of simplicity and depth… the father's fidelity to himself – a trait already known by the Old Testament *hesed* – is at the same time expressed in a manner particularly charged with affection.[226]

By tracing this theme of mercy through the scriptures Pope Saint John Paul II aims to reveal how rich in mercy God really is. He does this by linking God's faithfulness to the covenant with the father's compassion for his child: 'Mercy – as Christ has presented it in the parable of the prodigal son – has the interior form of the love that in the New Testament is called agape'.[227] This movement from *hesed* in the Old Testament to *agape* in the New is the manifestation of the 'mercy [which] constitutes the fundamental content of the messianic message of Christ and the constitutive power of His mission'.[228] Ironically

---

[225] Ibid, 5
[226] Ibid, 6
[227] Ibid
[228] Ibid

the rich meaning of this mercy will be further divined in another parable in which Jesus refers to a man described as *Dives*.

The Parable of the Rich Man and Lazarus

This is preceded in chapter 16 by the Parable of the Dishonest Manager who displays a degree of cunning to save his own skin by doing a series of deals with his master's debtors. Calling them together after he has been sacked he offers them varying degrees of debt forgiveness not out of a sense of solidarity or compassion but in an attempt to win favour with his boss. After closing with a reference to the master's commendation of the manager's shrewdness, Jesus makes a number of statements which lead the Pharisees 'who were lovers of money' (16:14) to ridicule him. Two of these are particularly significant in relation to the Parable of *Dives*[229] and Lazarus. The first of these – 'And I tell you, make friends for yourselves by means of dishonest wealth so that when it is gone, they may welcome you into the eternal homes' (16:9) – is not a complete condemnation of wealth but a commendation of almsgiving 'in the conviction that such sharing of possessions has a heavenly reward'[230]. The second – 'No slave can serve two masters; for a slave will either hate the one and love the other, or be devoted to the one and despise the other. You cannot serve God and wealth' (16:13) – illustrates the danger of idolatry, here investment in possessions instead of praise of God. The implications of these two sayings

---

[229] *Dives* is not a proper name but an adjective (in Latin) signifying someone who is rich. This is also applied as an attribute of God – as we have seen – in the encyclical *Dives in misericordia* (Rich in mercy).

[230] Johnson, *The Gospel of Luke*, 245

are interpreted by Johnson thus: 'If giving away possessions in almsgiving secures a place with God, the worship of possessions and a clinging to them as ultimate means separation from God'.[231]

The parable of *Dives* and Lazarus presents the contrasting fortunes of the two during their life on earth and after death. The rich man lives in splendour, wearing the best clothes money could buy and dining 'sumptuously every day' (16:19) while Lazarus is a poor man 'covered with sores' (16:20) who wanted to 'satisfy his hunger with what fell from the rich man's table (16:21). The detail of dogs coming to lick his sores highlights his distress and deepens the empathy of hearers. His situation is not unlike that of the son in the previous parable, except that there is no suggestion of responsibility for the sorry state Lazarus found himself in and which he could do nothing to alleviate or ameliorate. After death he is 'carried away to be with Abraham' (16:22) while *Dives* ends up in Hades, desperately pleading with Abraham to have mercy on him 'and send Lazarus to dip the tip of his finger in water and cool my tongue' (16:24). Denied this, he is reminded of the reversal of their respective fortunes during life and also of the present divide between them which cannot be closed in either direction. He is also denied his further plea to send Lazarus to warn his five brothers 'so that they will not come also into this place of torment' (16:28) on the basis that the teaching of Moses and the prophets is sufficient to save them from sharing a similar fate.

---

[231]   Ibid, 248

Noting that 'Luke's parable in 16:19-31 provides the perfect narrative expression of his own Beatitudes and woes in 6:20, 24' and offers 'only the divine reversal promised in the Sermon on the Plain', Johnson states that it is 'an appendix which complicates the simple story and gives it a polemic sting'.[232] Finding himself in Hades/Hell the once wealthy man cries out 'Father Abraham, have mercy on me' (16:24). This is the same appeal addressed to Jesus - later in *Luke* – by both the ten lepers (17:13) and the blind beggar who called out to him for mercy (18:39). This imprecation by all three invokes the divine mercy – *eleos* – indicated by Mary in the *Magnificat*. However, the difference between the request of *Dives* and the lepers/beggar is not simply down to the fact that they occur during life and after death but also due to the 'irony of the story that he now requests "mercy" (*eleos*) who did not show mercy in almsgiving (*ele□mosyn□*) to the poor man'.[233] This irony is intensified by the fact that 'the rich man cannot claim ignorance of the fact that someone hungry is outside his door, for he refers to Lazarus by name' and, moreover, indicates his continuing arrogance by his intercession 'that Abraham command Lazarus to come down and refresh him'.[234] However, the reason for Abraham's refusal of *Dives'* request for mercy is not only down to his attitude after death but related to his avarice during life. This is a graphic illustration of the evangelist's intention to indicate the importance and import of

---

[232]   Ibid, 256
[233]   Ibid, 252
[234]   Michael F. Patella, *The Gospel According to Luke* (Collegeville, MN: Liturgical Press, 2005), 111

Jesus' instruction on wealth and issues of inequality (involving in-justice) that arise in its wake.

From the beginning the evangelist expresses God's intentionality to identify with the destitute. Declaring that 'He has shown strength with his arm; he has scattered the proud in the thoughts of their hearts [and] He has brought down the powerful from their thrones, and lifted up the lowly '(1:51-52), the *Magnificat* lays the basis for what follows in Luke's account of Jesus' preferential option for the poor[235] and what is asked for from his followers in terms of possessing and sharing things. The opening of Jesus' ministry is presented through his proclamation of Isaiah's words (4:18-19) which announce that 'anointed as the Spirit-filled Christ/Messiah' Jesus 'is given a commission very much in keeping with the traditional role of the prophet in regard to the poor, the suffering and the marginalized'.[236] This option is the optic through which Jesus' own praxis must be perceived, particularly as he makes his own way to Jerusalem as the homeless prophet of God's Kingdom ('Foxes have holes, and birds of the air have nests; but the Son of Man has nowhere to lay his head', 9:58). Proclaiming the beatitude of the poor and hungry and how bereft the wealthy are, Jesus presents *Dives* and Lazarus in precisely these terms. As Johnson states:

---

[235] 'The Latin American theologians who first formulated the option for the poor believed that it was summoned forth by God's Word in the Scriptures...They relied on New Testament passages that announce the messianic mission of Jesus, especially his proclamation in the synagogue (Lk 4:18)'. Gregory Baum, *Amazing Church* (Maryknoll, New York: Orbis Books, 20050, 72-73

[236] Mullins, *The Gospel of Luke*, 169

The blessing of the poor and the rejection of the rich by God is sharply expressed in the story of Lazarus and the rich man...The story captures precisely the import of the first beatitude and woe found in Luke. We are not told explicitly that the rich man did anything bad in his lifetime (though from 16:19 and 31 the implication might be drawn that he did not practice alms-giving); he was just exceptionally rich. He had his consolation in this life (see 6:24) and after death he had to sit in Hades, bereft of comfort. Nor are we told that Lazarus was particularly virtuous. He was simply miserably poor in this life, and in the next life received his consolation, apparently for that reason alone (16:25).[237]

Daniel J. Harrington summarizes the message of the parable succinctly, 'as share what you have now, before it is too late'.[238] Moreover, reference to 'Moses and the prophets' in the parable not only roots Jesus' ministry and message in the tradition of their teaching about God's compassion for the poor but also requires his followers to read and heed them.[239] Thus Jesus, in the words of J. Philip Wogaman, 'makes clear that this teaching is fundamental to the whole Hebrew religious heritage'.[240] The corporate communication and command of this Biblical

---

[237] Luke Timothy Johnson, *Sharing Possessions – What Faith Demands*, 2nd ed (Cambridge, U.K.: Eerdmans, 2011), 14

[238] *Meeting St Luke Today* (Chicago: Loyola Press, 2009), 49

[239] See David L. Baker, 'Why Care for the Poor? Theological Foundations of Old Testament Laws on Wealth and Poverty', *Proceedings of the Irish Biblical Association*, 2007/No. 29, 1-20

[240] *Christian Ethics – A Historical Introduction*, 2nd ed (Louisville, Kentucky: Westminster John Knox Press, 2011), 15

heritage of helping the less fortunate is clearly enunciated by Amy-Jill Devine and Douglas Knight: 'Certainly not all widows were poor, and neither were all foreigners and orphans. But they were the most vulnerable members of the community. Rather than leave their care to the moral compass of those who were better off or to the compassionate individual, the law insists that all members of society bear responsibility for the care of its neediest members'.[241]

The parable is a prime example of Luke's theme of the 'great reversal', here expressed eschatologically with the respective fates of *Dives* and Lazarus fixed eternally. Saint Catherine of Siena gave the rich man no credit for begging Abraham to warn his brothers, writing that he did not wish 'to do them a good deed, but to prevent his suffering even more at their hands, should they end up where he is'.[242] Snodgrass' statement that 'the parable's eschatological relevance cannot be wiped away [and] the themes of reversal and judgement must be given their due'[243] brings the denial of *Dives'* plea for mercy to the fore. This raises the dialectic of divine forgiveness and human freedom which has been the subject of much theological debate down the centuries. One solution advanced has been Origen's theory of *apocatastasis* which 'argues that the fire of God's love rooted in the human and angelic creature cannot be extinguished and in the end consumes the sins of even the most

---

[241] Quoted in John W. Martens, 'The Word – God's Interest', *America*, 211 (20 October 2014), 43

[242] Harvey D. Egan, 'Hell: The Mystery of Eternal Love and Eternal Obduracy', *Theological Studies* 75(2014):52-73, here 70

[243] *Stories with Intent*, 432

hardened sinner'.[244] This answer has ironically not received universal theological approbation though Harvey D. Egan notes that 'the views of [Hans Urs Von] Balthasar and [Karl] Rahner, who hope that everyone will be saved, seem to dominate the contemporary theological horizon' and that 'it is striking, too, that the documents of Vatican II contain not a single reference to hell, even when speaking of eschatology'.[245] However, with the seeming absolute reversal and rejection of the rich man in the parable - symbolized by the 'great chasm' (16:26) and the refusal to grant his requests – Evans' comment (albeit on Luke 6:36-37) that 'this is awkward, since God's mercy cannot consist in his abjuring all judgements'[246] is apposite. David Lyle Jeffrey drives the point home:

> Abraham underscores not only the reversal of circumstances but also its unchangeable character. As if to acknowledge his privileged (but now futile) status, Abraham refers to him as "son", even as he explicates the justice in the reversal the rich man has suffered. Lazarus has been comforted at last; the rich man, though born a son of Abraham, failed to live up to his sonship and will never be comforted again (16:25). This story is very far from making a case for universal salvation; it is plainly aimed in the opposite direction, making a case consistently with what scripture says in many places about God's judgement

---

[244] Egan, 'Hell: The Mystery of Eternal Love and Eternal Obduracy', 60
[245] Ibid, 72
[246] *Saint Luke*, 337

on poor stewardship of wealth in the face of the poverty of others.[247]

Notwithstanding its eschatological reserve the ethical relevance of the parable is evident in the ever widening chasm between the wealthy and the poor in the world. The issue of inequality is increasingly commented on by economists and politicians, ethicists and social scientists. Moral theologian Kenneth Himes captures this reality in his '"Growing Apart": The Rise of Inequality' which opens with the straightforward statement that 'economic inequality is rising in the United States and across the globe'.[248] Among the keywords in this article are income distribution and wealth concentration. Focus on the so-called *über* wealthy is an increasing feature of media though John Kampfner states that 'our fascination and frustration with this era's super-rich is nothing new' as he 'explains what history teaches us about how people become wealthy .[249] Kampfner's reference to the 'Gospel of Wealth' brings Luke's interest in economic inequality to the fore:

> God's mercy on the physically hungry and economically poor is a major theme in Luke. This is true despite the valid point made by Luise Schottroff and Wolfgang Stegemann that, rather than calling Luke the evangelist of the poor, "one could with greater right call Luke the evangelist of the rich… in the sense that he is an extraordinarily sharp critic of the rich and is interested

---

[247] *Luke*, 204
[248] *Theological Studies*, 75(2014):118-132, here 118
[249] 'What makes the super-rich tick', *The Guardian*, 15 October 2014

in their repentance". It is true that much of the teaching about possessions in Luke is directed to those who have possessions, not the poor. Nevertheless, this teaching is motivated by a concern for the poor.[250]

In *The Joy of the Gospel* Pope Francis declares that 'God has shown the poor his "first mercy" and that this 'divine preference has consequences for the faith life of all Christians'.[251] Opting for 'a Church which is poor and for the poor'[252] and evoking the 'Church of the poor' expressed during the Second Vatican Council, he 'is not only addressing the Catholic world, but attempting to rally all people of good will against "unregulated capitalism" and for a renewed ethics to restore a more just world'.[253] While the social and structural implications of such a stance might seem to surpass the interpretation of the Parable of the Rich Man and Lazarus, Pope Francis' stated interest of 'only helping those who are in thrall to an individualistic, indifferent and self-centred mentality to be freed from those unworthy chains and to attain a way of living and thinking which is more humane, noble and fruitful'[254] servers to stir the conscience(s) of the descendants of *Dives* and his siblings. At 'a critical moment

[250] Robert C. Tannehill, *The Narrative Unity of Luke-Acts: A Literary Interpretation, Volume 1: The Gospel according to Luke* (Philadelphia: Fortress Press, 1986), 127-128

[251] *Evangelii Gaudium –The Joy of the Gospel* (Dublin: Veritas, 2013), 198

[252] Ibid

[253] Bruce Duncan, 'Pope Francis' Call for Social Justice in the Global Economy', *The Australasian Catholic Record,* 91 (April 2014):178-193, here 193. For a critique see Allister Heath, 'The Pope's a great man but you can't take his economic views as gospel', *The Daily Telegraph,* 11 June 2014.

[254] *Evangelii Gaudium –The Joy of the Gospel,* 208

in history for the Church to make a substantial contribution to rebuilding the moral foundations of economics and the whole process of globalization'[255] the timeliness of the parable is both truthful and tragic.

The Parable of the Pharisee and the Publican

Chapter 18 of *Luke* commences with the statement that 'Then Jesus told them a parable about their need to pray always and not to lose heart' (18:1) which introduces the *Parable of the Widow and the Unjust Judge* (18:2-8). This is followed by the present parable which Jesus addressed 'to some who trusted in themselves that they were righteous and regarded others with contempt' (18:9). Here Luke uses the pattern of the previous parable by contrasting two characters. While these do not engage in confrontation (concerning justice as in the case of the widow and judge) they exhibit and express conflicting approaches to prayer and pity. The Pharisee represents the type of those characterized by Jesus as being self-righteous and judgemental as, 'standing by himself' he gives thanks to God that he is not like others, 'even this tax-collector' (18:11) and concludes by commending his own regular fasting and tithing. The tax-collector does not refer to his fellow occupant of the temple but 'standing far off' and not raising his eyes towards heaven, 'was beating his breast and saying, "God, be merciful to me, a sinner!" (18:13).

Snodgrass interprets Luke's introduction to the parable as indicating that his interest is primarily with the Pharisee and his

---

[255]   'Pope Francis' Call for Social Justice in the Global Economy', 193

ilk because of Jesus' insistence that 'one cannot be obedient to God's Law without loving one's neighbour as oneself'.[256] The Pharisee's penchant for self-praise and dismissal of the Publican display a denial of the dovetailing of twin commandments of love of God and neighbour which Luke has portrayed in the parables of the *Compassionate Samaritan* and *Parent* with its contrast, in the latter, 'between the desperate and humble confession of the prodigal and the distancing and disdain of the elder brother'.[257] The Publican's posture and plea prove that he is not proclaiming his self-righteousness but providing 'the basis of the acquittal [which] is the tax collector's sense of his need, his throwing himself on the mercy of God, and the compassion of God who forgives sinners'.[258] This appeal (and acquittal) differs from Luke's other accounts of asking for mercy in three important aspects. Firstly, while the ten lepers and the blind beggar address Jesus (and *Dives* Abraham), here the tax-collector addresses God. Secondly, his asking for mercy is not a literal translation of the verb employed in these three expressions. Thirdly, he refers not only to his situation but to himself with his self-designation as a sinner.

Firstly, the tax-collector's appeal to God for mercy is more than a textual detail. In both the *Magnificat* and *Benedictus* mercy is the meaning and measure of God's dealing with His people, the core meaning of the covenant. Combining

---

[256]   *Stories with Intent*, 472

[257]   Ibid, 466

[258]   Ibid, 472 (However, Snodgrass adds that 'the basis of the acquittal of the tax collector is not expressed unless one takes v 14b as original with the parable'.)

faithfulness and forgiveness, mercy reveals the manner of God's relating, especially to those who repent. Theologically, this parable highlights the importance of prayer. Prayer is an important Lucan theme and Jesus is presented as one who both prays himself and encourages his disciples to do so too. Boivon's statement that 'Luke, as we know, insists on prayer'[259] underpins the place that the evangelist gives to prayer, particularly to perseverance in its practice. D.L. Bock brings out the heart of Luke's teaching: 'Prayer does not demand; it requests, humbly relying on God's mercy and will. It voices trust in God's care and provision of basic needs'.[260] This direct appeal to God discloses that mercy is not simply an attribute of God but that God is the source of such mercy. This address to God as the primary agent of mercy connects theology to Christology, disclosing God and dovetailing with the portrait of Jesus as the prophet of this divine compassion.

Secondly, by describing him as 'a twin of the prodigal son', Boivon declares that the publican 'considers himself to have nothing to his credit and hopes only to be the object of mercy'.[261] This estimation is expressed in the verb *hilaskomai*. Boivon brings out its meaning in this context:

In the passive, as here, it means 'be propitiated', 'be merciful', ' be gracious'. In the biblical tradition, which

---

[259] *Luke the Theologian*, 2nd Revised Edition (Waco, Texas: Baylor University Press, 2006), 453

[260] 'Gospel of Luke' in eds Joel B. Green and Scot McKnight, *Dictionary of Jesus and the Gospels*, Leicester, England: InterVarsity Press, 1992, p 509

[261] *Luke 2*, p 550

reversed the tradition of Greek religion, this passive implied an activity on God's own part rather than activity or piety on the part of human beings. By virtue of his grace and love, God agrees to be favourably disposed once more towards his people. The imperative 'be reconciled to me' (*hilastheti moi*)) is not exactly equivalent to 'have mercy on me' (*eleeson me*, 18:39). It suggests more the end of vindictiveness and the reestablishment of a relationship than compassion .[262]

Notwithstanding these nuances, modern translations into English regularly render the request of the tax-collector as asking for God's mercy. His plea echoes the prayer of the *Miserere*, 'Have mercy on me, O God, according to your steadfast love; according to your abundant mercy blot out my transgressions' (Ps 51:1). Consistent with the call of the ten lepers and that of the blind beggar, the tax-collector seeks spiritual healing, trusting in 'the tender mercy of God' (1:78). This parable, without parallel in Mark or Matthew, allows Luke to portray this divine mercy in practice that shows the power of salvation. As a preview of the encounter between Zacchaeus and Jesus who proclaims that he 'has come to call not the righteous but sinners to repentance' (5:32), Luke indicates that this salvation is manifestly present in the mission of Jesus.

Thirdly, this parable pronounces the juxtaposition of the righteous/repentant that Luke referred to earlier in the context of the parables of the lost and found – 'Just so, I tell you, there will be more joy in heaven over one sinner who repents than

---

[262]   Ibid

over ninety-nine righteous persons who need no repentance' (15:7). The self-stated righteousness of the Pharisee only serves to highlight the self-designation of the Publican as a sinner. Udo Schnelle's statement that 'Jesus' message of God's unconditional acceptance of human beings is made clear by *the turn to tax-collectors and sinners* in his own ministry'[263] is underpinned by the irony that the Publican combines consciously both tax-collector and sinner in his own person. Wilfrid J. Harrington contrasts the connected conceptions of self and God in the two characters of the parable:

> The Pharisee 'trusted in himself that he was righteous'; he was comfortable with his God. The sinner was not complacent. He had been branded an outcast, warned that God had no time for him. Yet his perception, unclouded by an all-too-human image of God, did discern the true God: 'God, be merciful to me, a sinner!' He had the honesty to look at himself, at his sorry state, his radical unworthiness. And he perceived that, notwithstanding this, God loved him.[264]

---

263   *Theology of the New Testament*, 104
264   *The Loving God* (Dublin: The Columba Press, 2012), 51

Chapter Six

Luke's Model of Mercy

'God's mercy also lay at the heart of Jesus' understanding of his mission as the one who proclaimed and enacted the kingdom of God'.[265]

'We do belong together; are members one of another. That does not mean that all our relationships are healthy, or that an important movement in moral life might not be resistance or challenge to the way things are. There are 'new things' to be born. Our belonging does mean, however, that we can never ultimately dismiss or abandon one another without at the same time diminishing ourselves. To be true to the deepest reality of our own lives means the willingness to be with and bear the reality of others despite, at times, the struggle and pain of it. Moral life is one of the arenas in which this compassionate relationship is expressed and made possible by the resurrection of Jesus'.[266]

Models of Christ

In assessing Luke's Christology, according to Ekaterini G. Tsalampouni, account must be taken of the particular approach adopted by Luke:

---

[265] Marianne Meye Thompson, 'Jesus and his God', in ed Markus Bockmuehl, *The Cambridge Companion to Jesus* (Cambridge: Cambridge University Press, 2001):41-55, here 49

[266] Sarah Bachelard, *Resurrection and Moral Imagination* (Surrey, U.K.: Ashgate, 2014), 118

> Luke's gospel is not a doctrinal treatise organized into thematic units like "Christology", "soteriology", "pneumatology", and so forth. Its theological ideas do not come to us directly and in a systematic way, but they are embedded within Luke's story in a way that is perhaps not entirely traceable any more. Thus, instead of a systematic theological discussion in Luke's Gospel, we could talk of a "narrative theology", that is, of the presence of particular theological notions and conceptions woven into a story.[267]

In accepting the plurality of approaches in Luke's Christology the remark of Beverly Roberts Gaventa is both apposite and reassuring: 'It is tempting to cast a glance at John 21:25 and plead that this essay canvass all the ways in which Luke identifies Jesus, an entire library shelf would not be able to contain it'.[268] Thus, the Christology of *Luke* cannot be articulated *tout court*. The mosaic like quality of Luke's Christology means that while he has, in the words of Robert F. O'Toole, 'a multifaceted description of Jesus', he 'surely emphasizes certain aspects; but he wants to present a complete portrait'. [269] While stating that 'the various titles and functions claimed by Jesus or ascribed to Jesus

---

[267] 'Jesus in the View of Luke' in eds Christos Karakolaês, Karl-Wilhelm Niebuhr and Sviatoslav Rogalsky, *Gospel Images of Jesus Christ in Church Tradition and in Biblical Scholarship* (Tübingen: Mohr Siebeck, 2012), 153-180, here 168

[268] 'Learning and Relearning the Identity of Jesus from Luke-Acts' in eds Beverly Roberts Gaventa and Richard B. Hays, *Seeking the Identity of Jesus – A Pilgrimage*, Cambridge, UK: Eerdmans, 2008. 148-165, here 164

[269] *Luke's Presentation of Jesus: A Christology* (Rome: Editrice Pontificio Instituto Biblico, 2004), 4

by others are obviously of considerable importance' Johnson insists that 'equally important are the modes of "showing" that are forms of indirect identification, such as the use of language echoing biblical stories in the construction of stories involving Jesus'.[270]

Here Luke's employment of the language of mercy/ compassion must be highlighted.

In a sentence that seems Lucan in its inspiration, the Second Vatican Council states that 'all have need of Christ who is the model, master, liberator, saviour, and giver of life'.[271] Located in the *Decree on the Church's Missionary Activity*, this typology articulates an array of approaches in aiming to advance key aspects of what the Council calls in its earliest document 'the mystery of Christ'[272]. These images are obviously inter-related. Thus the master must model what he teaches, witnessing to his words so as to be an example of his own wisdom. The integrity of Christ's instruction is included in his identity. As 'liberator' Christ looks to the healing of people from physical and psychological illness while as 'saviour' he leads them to repentance and conversion by setting them free through the forgiveness of their sins. As 'giver of life' he not only raises people from the dead, thereby restoring their earthly existence

---

[270] 'The Christology of Luke-Acts' in eds Mark Allan Powell and David R. Bauer, *Who Do You Say That I Am? – Essays on Christology* (Louisville, Kentucky: Westminster John Knox Press, 1999), 49-65, here 54

[271] *Decree on the Church's Missionary Activity*, 8, in *Vatican Council II – The Basic Sixteen Documents*, General Editor, Austin Flannery (Dublin: Dominican Publications, 2007)

[272] *Constitution on the Sacred Liturgy*, 2, in *Vatican Council II – The Basic Sixteen Documents*

but, through his own death and resurrection, is also the agent by which they receive the Holy Spirit and the gift of eternal life.

Each of these images could be employed in an exploration of Luke's presentation of the portrait of Jesus, chiefly (though not confined to) in his Gospel. One of Jesus' early appearances is his absence and subsequent discovery in the temple 'sitting among the teachers, listening to them and asking them questions' (2:46). *Magister* (in the conciliar text) can be translated as master/ teacher. It is interesting that Peter addresses him as both, 'Master' after the great catch of fish (5:5) and after Jesus says he has something to say to him, he replies receptively, 'Teacher, speak' (7:40). After a lawyer addresses him in reaction to the charge of hypocrisy made against the Pharisees – 'Teacher, when you say these things, you insult us too' (11:45) – Jesus rails against their own rigorism. A similar address by a Sadducee (20:28) receives a response by Jesus about the status of marriage post mortem which results in some of the scribes answering 'Teacher, you have spoken well' (20:39) and the editorial comment that 'they no longer dared to ask him another question' (20:40). As well as using contexts of conflict and controversy to capture the teaching of Jesus Luke presents its content directly, as in the Sermon on the Plain and, indirectly, through the parables. Tsalampouni states that of the 'significant motifs' in Luke's Christological composite 'is that of Jesus as an authoritative and powerful teacher'.[273]

As 'liberator' Luke looks to portray Jesus as practising what he preaches. Announcing the Reign of God, Jesus accompanies

---

[273] 'Jesus in the View of Luke', 172

it by his powerful actions to make it present in the lives of people. The inauguration of his ministry sees him interpreting the prophecy of Isaiah by incarnating it: "The Spirit of the Lord is upon me, because he has anointed me to bring good news to the poor. He has sent me to proclaim release to the captives and recovery of sight to the blind, to let the oppressed go free, to proclaim the year of the Lord's favour... Today this scripture has been fulfilled in your hearing" (4:18-21). This fulfilment puts the focus firmly on the present as, for Luke, 'Jesus is necessarily featured... as the one who, at the beginning of an episode "arrives" and becomes approachable once again, as the one who encounters the human needs and religious problems of living individuals, and, in these so-called "limit situations" brings again the experience of salvation, that is, a manifestation of divine mercy'.[274] Referring to Luke's reliance on and redaction of the prophetic text, Jon Sobrino states that 'far from spiritualizing Isaiah, Luke reinforces his realism' and 'that proclaiming the good news *to the poor* of this world cannot be a matter of words alone'.[275] Indeed the three words – *release*, *recovery* and *liberation* – that indicate Jesus' inauguration of his mission dictate his dealings with people who come to him seeking healing, help and hope. As the eschatological prophet Jesus seeks to entwine words and works in witnessing to the establishment of God's Reign and the emancipation of those

---

[274] Donald Senior, 'The Gospels and the Eucharist', in eds Vivian Boland and Thomas McCarthy, *The Word is Flesh and Blood* (Dublin: Dominican Publications, 2012), 76-87, here 84-85

[275] *Jesus the Liberator – A Historical-Theological View* (Maryknoll, New York: Orbis Books, 1993), 86-87

who suffer illness and injustice. Moreover, Luke is unapologetic in underlining how Jesus' efforts to liberate people from all forms of exclusion lead him to arouse the antagonism of the upholders of power, privilege and propriety.

In his detailed study of Luke's Christology O'Toole asserts that 'the evidence supports the conclusion that the dominant characteristic is Jesus as saviour'.[276] This 'dominant characteristic' dovetails with Luke's description of Jesus' liberating activity on behalf of those who are not well and women, the outcast and oppressed. Involving also sinners and their need for forgiveness, Luke's interpretation of salvation is integral, involving material, moral and spiritual dimensions of human life. Wendy Farley articulates this vision of salvation thus:

> All forms of brokenness call forth compassion, even the bentness of sin. There is an abandon that is proper to compassion...[which] the stories of Jesus' ministry suggest... His healing hand is remembered as extended to the excluded, poor, and sick, and to the sinful as well. He defends his ministry to society's morally handicapped by pointing out that "Those who are well have no need of a physician, but those who are sick; I have come to call not the righteous but sinners to repentance" (Lk 5:31-32)...The radicality of compassion is shown in the labour to redeem sinners and to liberate human beings from their own evil.[277]

---

[276]   *Luke's Presentation of Jesus: A Christology*, 4
[277]   *Tragic Vision and Divine Compassion – A Contemporary Theodicy*, (Louisville, Kentucky: Westminster/John Knox Press, 1990), 84-85

Luke connects the course of Jesus' journey to Jerusalem which culminates in his own death and resurrection with the achievement of salvation. As 'the "theologian of the way", [he] sees Jesus' way turning into the proclamation of the "way of salvation" for all who associate themselves with him'.[278] Jesus offers his own journey as the way to salvation to all who open themselves to his words and works and his witness to the will of God even – and especially – through the weakness of his own passion. Bearing salvation is not just a role, albeit the greatest, that Jesus plays but reveals who Jesus is, in relation both to God and humanity; as Sigurd Grindheim states:

> The acts of God insofar as they relate to human beings are performed by Jesus. Chief among these acts is the work of salvation, which Luke connects with Jesus to a much greater degree than the other Synoptic Gospels do. In Luke's Gospel, Jesus is not merely an agent of salvation; his role in salvation goes beyond that of bringing it. Salvation is connected with the person of Jesus himself.[279]

In contrast to John's more systematic treatment of the theme of life, Luke presents Jesus as the 'giver of life' through stories. The raising of the widow's son at Nain and the daughter of Jairus are, in the words of Bernard Sesboüé, 'extreme forms of healing' which 'are "messianic" proclamations of what the Messiah-Saviour is capable of doing and announce in

---

[278] Rudolf Schnackenburg, *Jesus in the Gospels – A Biblical Christology* (Louisville, Kentucky: Westminster John Knox Press, 1995), 163

[279] *Christology in the Synoptic Gospels – God or God's Servant?* (London:T&T Clark, 2012), 129

their own way what the saved world will be like, a world constituted by victory of life over death'.[280] This victory is achieved by Jesus' own death and resurrection, his 'paschal mystery [which] is the well-spring of life for the Church as well as the way to the fullness of life'.[281] Teresa Okure underlines its universality thus:

> Jesus gives his life so that believers in him may live. He offers eternal life, a participation in God's own unending life. In the biblical vision of this life, death is destroyed, the heavens and the earth are transformed, and God becomes the life principle of all peoples. No one is excluded from this divine life-giving mercy.[282]

Reference to the 'giver of life' shows the close connection between Jesus and the Holy Spirit who plays 'a role throughout Luke's story from the very beginning up to the last verses of the Gospel (24:29) and continues to play a role in the book of Acts.'[283] Variously described by Luke as 'full of the Spirit' (4:10) and 'filled with the power of the Spirit', (4:14), he exemplifies life in the Spirit and empowers his disciples to be(come) like him.

---

[280] *The Resurrection and the Life* (Collegeville, MN: The Liturgical Press, 1996), 24
[281] Anthony Cernera, 'The Celebration of Our Paschal Liberation', *The Way*, 24 (1984): 224-238, here 235
[282] 'The global Jesus' in *The Cambridge Companion to Jesus*, 237-249, here 246
[283] 'Jesus in the View of Luke', 175

'An example for all ages'[284]

The first of the (five) models or titles given to Christ in the conciliar text refers to Christ as 'exemplar'. In the experience of his earliest disciples encounter with Jesus may have initially involved witnessing the way(s) in which he interacted with people. Whether as exemplar or educator or most probably combining elements of both the disciples came to confess Jesus as liberator, saviour and giver of life. Addressing his disciples prior to his ascension as 'witnesses of these things' (Lk 24:48) the Risen Jesus remains a model for all to whom the Gospel is proclaimed. Saint Irenaeus' image of Christ as 'example for all ages' is obviously intended as an ongoing invitation for people of 'all nations' (Lk 24:47) to imitate him. The typology of Christ as the exemplar of the Christian life is not a theological tautology but an image which integrates the imitation of Christ (*imitatio Christi*) with Christ as the icon of God. For Richard A. Burridge, Luke 'is the evangelist who makes the role of *mimesis*, imitation, most explicit'.[285] However, Peter W. Gosnell insists that 'Luke does not portray Jesus urging his followers to do exactly as he did but 'instead, Luke shows a pattern of living'.[286]

This pattern of living, dying and rising provides the template whereby, in the words of William C. Spohn, 'through

---

[284] Saint Irenaeus, quoted in Peter Bouteneff, 'Christ and Salvation' in eds Mary B. Cunningham and Elizabeth Theokritoff (*The Cambridge Companion to Orthodox Christian Theology*, Cambridge: Cambridge University Press, 2008), 93-106, here 99

[285] *Imitating Jesus – An Inclusive Approach to New Testament Ethics* (Cambridge, UK: Eerdmans, 2007), 280

[286] *The Ethical Vision of the Bible – Learning Good from Knowing God* (Downers Grove, Illinois: IVP Academic, 2014), 193

faithful imagination his story becomes paradigmatic for moral perception, disposition, and identity'.[287] Wolfgang Schrage summarizes the standard set by Luke:

> The third evangelist demonstrates by the life of Jesus what true Christian life looks like... It is thus no accident that all the *example stories* in the New Testament are found in the Gospel of Luke. The stories of the Rich Fool, of the Good Samaritan, of the Rich Man and Poor Lazarus and the Pharisee and the Tax Collector are models of right and wrong conduct intended directly to motivate the Church to step over cultural boundaries with compassion, not to base its life on material possessions, and to practise genuine humility in relation to both God and other human beings.[288]

In his presentation of 'Jesus Christ, the Pattern', James M. Gustafson states that 'the full meaning of Christ for moral life escapes us if we make him exclusively a pattern, just as it does if he becomes exclusively the Redeemer-Lord, the Sanctifier, or the Justifier'.[289] For Gustafson, promoting Christ as *Pattern* means distinguishing between him as 'example' and 'moral ideal' as he is 'not all-sufficient as a source of moral guidance'.[290] Claiming that Christ 'is the *Pattern* in the sense that his life was

---

[287] *Go and Do Likewise – Jesus and Ethics* (New York: Continuum, 1999), 2

[288] *The Ethics of the New Testament* (Philadelphia: Fortress Press, 1988), 509-510

[289] *Christ and the Moral Life* (New York: Harper & Row, 1968), 181. Gustafson also devotes individual chapters to 'Jesus Christ, The Lord Who Is Creator And Redeemer/The Sanctifier/The Justifier/The Teacher'.

[290] Ibid, 187

the exhibition, expression, and manifestation of his Godliness', Gustafson goes on to explain the sense in which he is exemplar: 'Our lives in faith partake of his Godliness, and like his can manifest, express and exhibit moral seriousness and moral action, self-denial, cross-bearing, and love as the fruits of God's work'.[291] To perceive Christ properly as *Pattern* presupposes participation through faith in his paschal mystery. Conformity to Christ is created by interior conversion and not by uniformity with an exterior ideal. 'The fruits of God's work' flow from being formed by the Holy Spirit to follow the example of Christ. By his invitation to imitation 'Jesus was calling those who had experienced the mercy of God to make it the motivation and measure of their action as well'.[292]

Luke develops his narrative through the journeys he describes, Mary's visit to Elizabeth, Jesus going up to Jerusalem. Even after his Resurrection Luke relates how Jesus walked with two of his disciples to Emmaus. The way that Jesus walks is more than a metaphor, much like a map laying out the moral and spiritual route to be followed. In his outreach to others and obedience to God Jesus prepares and points out the paschal way of salvation. This way is his example which is shown and seen in the goodness he exhibits and the holiness he embodies, through the suffering he endures and the salvation he effects. For Luke Jesus is the exemplar who exceeds all others in his example on earth of the mystery and mercy of God. If 'Example' might seem too static a concept to capture the dynamic interplay

---

[291] Ibid
[292] Thompson, 'Jesus and his God', 50

of interaction and intervention involved in Jesus' inauguration of the Reign of God, it could be complemented by the character of 'Witness' to reflect the catalytic character of his ministry and resonate more with present day experience. As a witness to what God wants both for and from people, Jesus expresses in words and works the will of God. His integrity is intimately involved in his example and ultimately inseparable from his identity as exemplar:

> Jesus not only preaches the love, goodness, justice, compassion and incalculable mercy and faithfulness of God, but *is* that love, goodness, justice, compassion, mercy, and faithfulness in person. Christians have faith in Christ because he only talks about a new and better way of being human, but also reveals and embodies it in everything he does. Christians focus their lives on Christ because it is impossible for them to distinguish what they believe from who they believe; in other words, in his whole way of being in the world, in his attitudes, emotions, words and actions, Jesus verifies what he testifies.[293]

Noting that 'Luke explicitly presents Jesus as the ethical model and teacher for his disciples and (future) followers' Paula Fredriksen states that 'nowhere does Jesus shine more as a moral exemplar than in the final stages of his ministry, as he suffers abuse in silence and prays for his tormentors'.[294] The

---

[293] Paul J. Waddell, 'Christology and the Christian Life', *Journal of Moral Theology*, 2 (2013), 1-23, here 8

[294] *From Jesus To Christ – The Origins of the New Testament Images of Jesus*, London: Yale University Press, 1988, 30

passion of Jesus according to Luke portrays a figure of patient endurance who exemplifies forgiveness by healing the slave of the high priest struck by Peter and forgiving Peter himself for his betrayal. Jesus' example of suffering and forgiveness exceeds an ethical model as, leading by example to the end, he lays down his life in his self-emptying sacrifice on the cross. Thus, Jonathan R. Wilson states that 'this image of Christ as an example for humankind is tied to his way of life, particularly his sacrificial way of life [which] is most clearly seen in his death, but sacrifice, laying down his life, also involves Jesus' whole way of living'.[295] Unlike the stoic exemplar of cold or, in contemporary code, cool detachment Jesus does not stand or set himself apart from others but devotes his life to service and suffering for the sake and salvation of others.

An interesting feature of Luke's illustration of Jesus as exemplar is his use of stories in which Jesus points to the example of others, either holding them up as models to be imitated or ignored. Two stories set side by side show this contrast clearly. In the first Jesus instructs his disciples 'In the hearing of all the people...[to] beware of the scribes' (20:45-46). Among the reasons given for wariness around them are their affectation and avarice. The charge that 'they devour widows' houses and for the sake of appearance say long prayers' is a criticism of their hypocrisy. By exploiting their education and position they fail to observe the decencies of duty and devotion, desiring only to maintain their lavish lifestyle and love of adulation. Given

---

[295]   *God So Loved the World – A Christology for Disciples,* Grand Rapids, Michigan: Baker Academic, 2001, 119

the prominence placed by Jesus on prayer and protection of the poor it is not surprising to be able to reach the verdict 'that they will receive the greater condemnation' (20:47). In the second Jesus contrasts the sight of the rich contributing to the Temple treasury with 'a poor widow put[ting] in two small coins' (21:2). Asserting his moral and spiritual authority he declares that she has given 'more than all of them' because 'out of her poverty [she] has put in all she had to live on' (21:4). Noting that this story 'comes shortly before the passion narrative' Barbara E. Reid comments that 'the widow who gives her whole life prefigures Jesus' own handing over of his very life on behalf of others'.[296] The intention of inserting the story of the widow's sacrifice is to invite 'the hearer to do the same'.[297] Thus the evangelist echoes the exhortation at the end of the *Parable of the Compassionate Samaritan* to 'Go and do likewise'.

Jesus, the Compassionate One

In his examination of biblical models of evangelization Marcel Dumais differentiates between those which have the apostles and Jesus as agents of mission.[298] Among those approaches attributed to Jesus, Dumais gives an account of 'The Evangelical Model of Humanism' which he analyses in terms of 'the exemplary quality of his life on earth and the programme of life and happiness that he proposes'.[299] He articulates the

---

[296] *Choosing the Better Part? Women in the Gospel of Luke* (Collegeville, Minnesota: The Liturgical Press, 1996), 195-196

[297] Ibid

[298] *After Emmaus – Biblical Models for the New Evangelization* (Collegeville, 'Minnesota: The Liturgical Press, 2014), Chapter 4, 58-78

[299] Ibid, 58

first of these through an analysis of some passages from *Luke* which portray the humanist approach adopted by Jesus in his interaction with people in general and invitation to individuals to become his disciples. His answer to the question 'Who then is Jesus?' is: 'Jesus is a man of compassion, a man of immense compassion. And his compassion is a reflection of the compassion of God the Father. Through his humanity, marked profoundly by compassionate love, Jesus reveals the love of God the Father for all human beings'.[300] The compassionate humanity of Jesus is heralded by Luke and held up as the hallmark of discipleship: 'Luke gives us a profound understanding of the message of his gospel in three stories, the central message of which is expressed by the use of a single Greek verb *esplagnisthè*. In this gospel, this verb is used only in these stories, which have no parallels in the other gospels'.[301] Dumais declares that Christian discipleship 'manifests for those who are suffering the kind of compassion that was present in Jesus at the moment of his encounter with the widow of Nain, the compassion that was present in the Samaritan for the man left half dead, the compassion that was present in the father of the prodigal son'.[302]

The characterization of the compassionate heart of Jesus in *Luke* is also communicated through a number of events that are found only in this Gospel. The sight of Jesus weeping over Jerusalem – 'As he drew near and came in sight of the city he shed tears over it' (19:41) – is accompanied by his statement – 'If you too had only recognized on this day the way to peace!'

---

[300]   Ibid, 64
[301]   Ibid
[302]   Ibid, 72

(19:42). Echoing the words of the *Benedictus* – 'to guide our feet into the way of peace' – Luke connects the journey of Jesus to Jerusalem with the coming of God and the consequence of failing to accept the offer of salvation contained therein. The pathos of these lines transcends the previous lament where Jesus longed 'to gather your children together, as a hen gathers her brood under her wings' (13:34). Referring to the 'prophetic prehistory' of this plaintive scene, Robert J. Karris quotes that it is 'the sympathy of the suffering prophet, of Deuteronomy's Moses, of Jeremiah, Isaiah, and Hosea, caught up in the rage, anguish, frustration, and sorrow of God for Israel that constitutes the pathos of this story'.[303] As this latter lament leads Jesus into Jerusalem from where he will emerge as a criminal condemned to the way of the cross, his cry is not one of condemnation but compassion for all those in the city. Thus Luke reiterates that 'the God of Jesus is never vengeful but always compassionate'.[304]

On the way to Calvary he encounters some women 'who mourned and lamented for him' (23:27). Reversing the encounter with the widow at Nain, Jesus is now seen as the one standing in need of mercy and comfort or in the case of Simon of Cyrene's assistance, falling. In complete contrast to the callous cruelty of his captors and the brutality of the crowd baying for his blood, the women cry out compassionately at the sight of Jesus in the last steps of his journey. Mullins sees Jesus as turning 'the[ir] sympathy away from himself'[305] as he

---

[303] *The Gospel of Luke*, in *The New Jerome Biblical Commentary*, 712
[304] Anthony Gittins, 'For the Wind Was Against Them (Mk 6:48), *The Australasian Catholic Record*, 92 (2015):41-52, here 49
[305] *The Gospel of Luke*, 495

addresses these 'Daughters of Jerusalem', advising them not to weep for him but rather for yourselves and for your children' (23:28). The dramatic effect of his words to them about the fate of Jerusalem and future generation(s) is deepened by the (recent) memory of his own tearful lament over the city. While there is no doubting the generally ominous and obviously apocalyptic air of his address, the gentle tone adopted by Jesus indicates that it is not an admonition intended to threaten the women or their families. This is in keeping with his demeanour throughout and displays his compassionate appreciation of their tears and terror.

Jesus' final exchange prior to expiring is with one of the two criminals who were executed with him. After the other cynically, albeit in the circumstances ironically, repeatedly asks Jesus about being the Christ and his ability to save all three of them, he is rebuked by the one who reiterates the innocence of Jesus and the injustice of his crucifixion. Karris comments that 'the criminal has deep faith that the dying Jesus is truly a king and can dispense the pardon and mercy which only a king can'.[306] After asking Jesus to receive him into his kingdom, he is assured that his destination after death the same day is heaven. This incident enables the evangelist to express editorially at the end of Jesus' life the contrasting responses he has experienced in the course of his life. However, Jesus does not respond to the ridicule of the thief who rejects him but to the recognition of the one who repents. As Patella states, 'at this point Jesus

---

[306] *The Gospel of Luke*, 719

again utters words of mercy'.[307] Having already pardoned his persecutors and executioners, Jesus now mediates with messianic authority – 'Truly, I tell you, today you will be with me in Paradise' (23:43) – the forgiveness of God for this sinner. For Fitzmyer, 'Luke makes use of this third scene of mockery to let it become a manifestation of mercy'.[308] The words of Jesus to Zacchaeus – 'I must stay at your house today' (19:5) – are transposed to transport this prodigal son of Abraham to the home of the heavenly Father into whose hands Jesus commends his own spirit.

The sensitivity shown by Jesus in these scenes reveals his extraordinary solidarity with people, even – and especially – in the course of his own extreme suffering. It is this 'closeness to human beings' that characterizes Luke's portrayal of Jesus, constituting for Schnackenburg 'Jesus' humane quality' which 'stands out above his humanity'. [309] As McDermott observes, 'the Lucan Jesus of the ministry is given the most human and appealing portrait in the Gospels'.[310] Often noted and quoted for his artistic inclination the Lucan portrayal of Jesus is particularly appealing because of the way he interacts with people, responding to their requests for all kinds of help, ready to intervene on their behalf. In presenting Jesus in this way the evangelist installs him as the original icon and instrument of God's mercy, inculcating intercession for mercy, human and

---

307 *The Gospel According to Luke*, 150
308 *The Gospel According to Luke (X-XXIV)*, 1509
309 *Jesus in the Gospels – A Biblical Christology*, 183
310 *Word Become Flesh – Dimensions of Christology*, 73

divine. Michael Amaladoss draws out the implications of seeing Jesus as the incarnation of divine mercy:

> The image of the compassionate Jesus also highlights aspects of solidarity in the process of salvation. To the gift of God corresponds our faith Compassion which, like freedom in dialogue, is a two-way process. It humanizes the salvific relationship, unlike salvific paradigms that are based on metaphors of redemption or punishment. Jesus the compassionate is indeed *Emmanuel* – God with us.[311]

Towards a Christology of Compassion

A complete Christology of *Luke* is beyond the scope of this study, not least for the fact that it would have to take account of the titles attributed to Jesus throughout even if, as O'Toole acknowledges, 'there is some truth to the statement that Luke mingles the meanings of titles with one another'.[312] Nevertheless, it is hoped that concentrating on Luke's expressions of mercy would help us conceive how they coalesce in his characterization of Jesus' identity vis-à-vis relationship with God and others and thereby contribute to seeing his composite portrait of Jesus. In this endeavour support is taken from the statement of Wilfrid Harrington that 'at any rate, the Christ of Luke is throughout,

---

[311] *The Asian Christ* (Maryknoll, New York: Orbis Books, 2006), *Chapter 9/ Jesus, the Compassionate*, 135-146, here 146

[312] *Luke's Presentation of Jesus: A Christology,* 2. Also, as McDermott avers, 'a full appreciation of Lucan theology and Christology requires a reading of the third gospel and the Acts of the Apostles as a two-volume work by a single author'. *Word Become Flesh*, 72-73

and before all else, a Saviour who is full of compassion and tenderness and great forgiveness'.[313] Acknowledging that '"loving mercy" or "compassion" can be an attribute both of God and of Jesus [as] they are concerned to save' O'Toole asserts that 'God works his loving mercy through Jesus, or Jesus' own compassion brings someone salvation'.[314]

Thus John R. Donahue links the compassion of God with the coming of Jesus. This is the 'day' declared by Zechariah when 'by the tender mercy of our God the dawn from on high will break upon us' (1:78): 'the compassion of God stands behind the coming of Jesus, just as in Exodus 3:7-8 the Lord comes to the aid of the suffering people of Israel, after seeing their affliction, hearing their cries, and knowing their sufferings'.[315] For Donahue 'compassion is that divine quality which, when present in human beings, enables them to share deeply in the sufferings and needs of others and enables them to move from one world to the other: from the world of helper to the one needing help; from the world of the innocent to that of the sinner'.[316] More than a phenomenological description of compassion, this is a theological depiction of divine mercy. Moreover, in his analysis of the parable of the Good Samaritan he declares that 'under Luke's tutelage the parable becomes *a paradigm of the compassionate vision* which is the presupposition for ethical action'.[317] If the parable of the Good Samaritan provides

---

[313]   'Birth of Christ', *Spirituality*, 20 (2014), 341-347, here 347
[314]   *Luke's Presentation of Jesus: A Christology*, 71
[315]   *The Gospel in Parable* (Minneapolis: Fortress Press, 1988), 132
[316]   Ibid
[317]   Ibid

this paradigm then Jesus is shown by Luke as the model who personifies the vision of God's mercy.

Jon Sobrino states that 'the principle that seems to us to be the most "structuring" of all, as we examine Jesus' life, is the element of *mercy* in that life'.[318] Examining 'Jesus' life' through 'the element of *mercy*' is especially valid and extremely valuable for reading *Luke*. The evangelist employs *mercy* as the structuring principle to present the life of Jesus, in the words of McDermott, as 'the compassionate, Spirit-led prophet who opts for the poor, the marginalized, and the broken in mind and body'.[319] Mercy was his meaning and Luke's 'Life of Jesus' is structured narratively and normatively in terms of that mission and message. While not referring explicitly to *Luke*, Sobrino's statement could serve as an excellent summary of how this Gospel structures its account of the life of Jesus: 'Mercy is not the sole content of Jesus' practice, but it is mercy that stands at the origin of all that he practices; it is mercy that shapes and moulds his entire life, mission, and fate. Sometimes the word mercy appears explicitly... and sometimes it does not'.[320]

While *mercy* is not explicitly mentioned in the story of Jesus meeting with the two disciples as they make their way to Emmaus it is evident throughout the encounter and the experience of those who had taken what the women told them earlier as 'an idle tale' (24:11). Luke's statement that 'Jesus himself came near and went with them' (24:15) communicates the closeness

---

[318]   *The Principle of Mercy* (Maryknoll, New York: Orbis Books, 1994), 15-16
[319]   *Word Become Flesh – Dimensions of Christology*, 73
[320]   *The Principle of Mercy*, 19-20

to people that has been characteristic of his ministry. On this occasion he is content to ask them what they are talking about, at which point they stand still 'looking sad' (24:17). The irony of identifying Jesus as 'the only stranger in Jerusalem who does not know the things that have taken place there in these days' (24:18) is intensified by the patience of his reply which allows them to list their frustration and sense of failure in following him. While acknowledging him as 'a prophet mighty in deed and word before God and all the people' they also articulate they 'had hoped that he was the one to redeem Israel' (24:21). Despite their lack of understanding and even unbelief, Marcel Dumais, OMI discerns that the approach Jesus adopts here is that of meeting 'people where they are on the journey' and listening 'to them as they express their concerns, their suffering, and their disappointments'.[321] Dumais discerns that the attitude of Jesus to the distress of the disciples is akin to 'the parable of the Good Samaritan from this same Gospel of Luke' which 'is an invitation to compassion, and more specifically an invitation to see the[ir] interior wounds'.[322]

Luke presents the risen Jesus on the road to Emmaus as merciful, not moralistic. Having listened to the complaints of Cleopas and his companion, Jesus responds by saying 'how foolish' and 'slow of heart to believe all that the prophets have declared!' (24:25). This is more a lamentation than a lambasting, a *cri de coeur* rather than a condemnation. His stance is similar to that he had taken as he stood before and

---

[321] *After Emmaus*, 94
[322] Ibid, 95

cried for the city which became the scene of the sad things the two disciples have spoken of and perhaps cried over in his presence. David Lyle Jeffrey comments that 'as so often, Jesus' most gentle teaching and self-disclosure begins with a rebuke; it is a more gentle rebuke than many of the translations readily suggest'.[323] The risen Jesus is not concerned with setting the record straight by reproving the two disciples before him. There is no touch of triumphalism in his tone but tenderness as he tells them the truth about the suffering and glorification of God's Messiah, interpreting 'to them the things about himself in all the scriptures' (24:27).

Having reached their destination the disciples press Jesus strongly to stay with them 'because it is almost evening and the day is now nearly over' (24:29). This detail recalls another event earlier in *Luke* when as 'the day was drawing to a close' (9:12) the twelve came to Jesus and urged him to send the crowd away to find food and shelter. Then, 'taking the five loaves and the two fish, he ... blessed and broke them, and gave them to the disciples to set before the crowd' (9:16). The same sequence of actions over the bread in Emmaus also recalls the last supper and reveals the identity of the stranger to his two table companions. Jesus shows here the supreme manifestation of 'the tender mercy' that Zechariah spoke about, which gives light to the darkness of the disciples and guides their 'feet into the way of peace' (1:79). After the denouement of their encounter with Jesus there is a mutual realization that their hearts were inflamed as he interpreted the scriptures for them. By moving

---

[323]   *Luke*, 285

from mention of their 'sad faces' to 'their burning hearts' Luke expresses metaphorically their experience of 'the salvation Jesus brings as "light", "grace" and "loving mercy"'.[324] The detail of their returning to Jerusalem 'that same hour' (24:33) recalls their earlier request to Jesus to remain with them and highlights what has happened to them. Having fled from that place they now return in faith, freed from their fears and failures, to tell 'the eleven and their companions gathered together' (24:33) that the risen Lord has appeared to them too.

In a chapter entitled 'Jesus – The Person', Frederick W. Danker gives a formulation in which a reader of *Luke* can fittingly frame a *Christology of Compassion*:

> What Jesus said and did was of a piece with what he was intrinsically as a person – totally and radically committed to Yahweh's will and purpose and to the liberation of people. That unique aspect of his *life* was of such interest to Luke that it serves as the nerve centre for his total Christological construct. For the future of Christianity depended, so far as Luke was concerned, on fidelity to the radicality in Jesus' own personal style of life, word, and action. But in that very radicality there were depths of human expression of such admirable quality that they would appeal to gentile admirers of the highest virtues, who might otherwise have had little interest in the subtler points of theology.[325]

---

[324]   *Luke's Presentation of Jesus: A Christology*, 227
[325]   *Luke*, 2nd Edition (Fortress Press, Philadelphia: 1987), 100

The radicality of Jesus' life is his relationship to Yahweh, to the God he knew intimately and uniquely as 'Father'. His life is rooted in fully and faithfully representing his Father by his mission of revealing God's Reign of mercy which means salvation for people. The course of Jesus' journey is composed of events and encounters which educate his disciples that he is completely committed to 'the liberation of people'. By communicating 'the depths of human expression' in his portrayal of Jesus Luke is capable of attracting people to admire and ask about his identity. The quality that Luke concentrates on in his characterization of Jesus is compassion. This is communicated again and again in the concern that Jesus showed for the sick and poor, to those who were outcast and even outlawed. Combining a complete consistency of attitude, articulation and action Jesus is clad by Luke, in an image borrowed from another evangelist, in a seamless garment of compassion. Communicating the mercy of God which he calls on his followers to copy, the radicality of his life and death is inseparably connected to its quality. Desiring to depict Jesus as Son of the 'Most High,' Luke's portrait presents him as the Son of Mercy. It is thanks to this evangelist 'that the Christian God is understood to be preeminently a God of mercy who needs little elaboration'.[326]

Jesus as God's Compassion

Monika K. Hellwig aims to build a Christology for contemporary Christians centred on the compassionate

---

[326] James P. Hanigan, *As I Have Loved You – The Challenge of Christian Ethics* (New York: Paulist Press, 1986), 218. See also Donald J. Goergen, *The Compassionate Sage/Chapter 7* in *The Mission and Ministry of Jesus*, Vol. 1 (Wilmington, Delaware: Michael Glazier, 1986)

message and ministry of Jesus. Among the characteristics of Jesus highlighted by the evangelists she notes 'his ready and immense compassion for any kind of suffering'.[327] Her reference to Jesus' reason for leaving Nazareth as being rooted in 'compassion for the alienated' recalls his image of the father who shows mercy for his wayward son in Luke 15 and his insistence that 'the true tragedy in human affairs is not that there is a history of sin and alienation, but that redemptive compassion and true empathy have died out in the experience of those who claim to live in the father's house and to be about the father's business'.[328] This 'business' is to bring the Reign of God to bear on situations of human brokenness so as to build up and bind the wounds of sickness and sinfulness, to break down the barriers and borders between people as suggested strongly in the Parable of the Compassionate Samaritan. As the bearer of salvation Jesus both proclaims and makes present 'the compassionate yearning of God for the reconciliation and peace of his human creation'.[329] Jesus receives two responses from people, one of grateful acceptance, the other of grudging refusal. Not daunted by the negativity of those who reject his message because of their vacuous ignorance or vested interests, 'the compassion of Jesus grows to boundless proportions in that he continues his healing and rebuilding ministry where he can'[330] despite its personal cost which culminates in his passion and crucifixion.

---

[327] *Jesus –The Compassion of God* (Dublin: Dominican Publications, 1983), 78
[328] Ibid, 81
[329] Ibid, 82
[330] Ibid, 84

The cross of Jesus is not a 'compensation paid to God for the offence to God's majesty expressed in human sinning'[331] but the condescension of His Christ in the offering of divine mercy.

Hellwig maintains that it is 'the many-faceted compassion of Jesus that offers the key to the Resurrection'.[332] This compassion not only reaches out 'to every kind of human suffering both in healing and in challenge' but 'redeems the situation of hopelessness'.[333] This involvement of Jesus and intervention of God reveals power as pathos and converts control into compassion. She concludes the chapter entitled 'The Resurrection of Jesus and the Imitation of Christ' by dovetailing assertion and appeal:

> In the total self-gift of his compassion, Jesus acts most divinely, yet it is in the same compassion that he becomes in his Resurrection most imitable. To be a follower of Jesus means in the first place to enter by compassion into his experience, with all that it expresses of the divine and of the human. And it means in the second place to enter with him into the suffering and the hope of all persons, making common cause with them as he does, and seeking out as he does the places of his predilection among the poor and despised and oppressed.[334]

For Hellwig 'the Compassion of God' is characteristic of the divine activity in relation 'to the creation and to creatures

---

[331] Ibid, 97
[332] Ibid,107
[333] Ibid
[334] Ibid, 108

as well as to the redemption of the human race and its history'.[335] Embodying entirely God's entry on earth, Jesus' identity is absolutely involved in this activity. His outreach is ultimately the offer of salvation which, on the one hand, shows solidarity with human suffering and, on the other, liberation from human sinfulness. The genius of *Luke* is the opportunity it gives to observe God's characteristic compassion operating in the merciful ministry of Jesus to the point of his complete self-offering. Thus Carl R. Holladay refers, in his commentary on *The Gospel of Luke*, to Jesus 'practicing uncalculating mercy'.[336] That a Christology of compassion can be conceived is indisputable; that it can be constructed is invaluable; that it can be communicated is indispensable; that it cannot be counted or costed is immeasurable.

---

[335]   Ibid, 122-123

[336]   *A Critical Introduction to the New Testament – Interpreting the Message and Meaning of Jesus Christ* (Nashville: Abingdon Press, 2009), 181

Chapter Seven

Making a Virtue of Mercy

'In compassion the self experiences the other... as another who suffers and whose sufferings become not our own, since they are always recognized as being the suffering of another, but become the cause of our action as if they were our own'[337]

'"Be compassionate as God is compassionate", Jesus said. In this short verse, theology and ethics are combined in a few words'.[338]

'Scripture's most important role is not in resolving crisis points but in training us to respond at the right time in the right way to the situations in which we find ourselves'[339]

Return to Virtue(s)

The renewal of moral theology in the past five to six decades has seen a return to reflection on virtue at the root of Christian moral living. This recovery of the virtues in moral theology resulted from the debate and disagreement about the identity of

---

[337] Oliver Davies, *A Theology of Compassion* (London: SCM Press, 2001), xix

[338] Marcus J. Borg, 'Jesus Before and After Easter' in eds Marcus J. Borg, N.T. Wright, *The Meaning of Jesus –Two Visions* (London: SPCK, 2003), 53-78, here 70

[339] Angus Paddison, *Scripture: A Very Theological Proposal* (London: T&T Clark, 2009), 39-40

Christian morality which dominated the discipline in the 1970s and 1980s. This focus allows moral theologians to found their subject specifically in terms of the relationship of the theological and moral virtues. This structured relationship of theology and morality traces the ways in which the infused virtues inform and influence the moral or cardinal virtues. A theology of the virtues tracks across time the trajectory of conversion in terms of how faith, hope and charity shape the moral life of the followers of Christ. By asking, for example, how charity shapes the obligations and outcomes of justice or how hope can challenge or contribute to courage, a theological ethic of the virtues explores the interaction of grace and nature in the formation of Christian moral character and its fruit(s) in conduct. Interest in the virtues is also reflected in increasing investigation of the relationship between morality and spirituality, directed towards the dovetailing of the divine draw to holiness and the human drive to goodness.

The renewed interest in the Bible by moral theologians in recent decades has resulted in the removal of over reliance on one scriptural text, the Commandments. This over reliance obscured the significance of the virtues which are no strangers to the scriptures, both Hebrew and Christian. Readings in the Mass for the Dead regularly refer to virtue as in the familiar versions from the Book of Wisdom: "The souls of the virtuous are in the hands of God' (3:1) and 'The virtuous man, though he dies before his time, will find rest' (4:7). The psalmist regularly plays off virtue against vice, particularly in the personification of the upright against the underhand. Paul employed this method more extensively in his exposition of lists of vice and virtue.[340] Commenting on the Bible as a source of virtue Lúcás Chan states that 'some scholars, following Athanasius' word that "the entire Holy Scripture is a teacher of virtues" claim that the moral agenda found in Scripture is written in terms of virtue'.[341] Investigating moral identity and interpreting ethical insight in terms of the virtues has become a collaborative venture for moral theologians and scripture scholars.[342] The Council's call for moral theology to draw 'more fully on the teaching of holy scripture' finds fertile ground in the field of the virtues and their frequency in the Bible. Attention to and analysis of the virtue narratives in scripture helps to see the holistic and historical dynamic of discipleship. Moreover, a theological virtue ethics supports the vital link between spirituality and morality. By focussing on the primacy of persons over the priority of precepts and the formation of the faithful in the virtues moral theology highlights their 'lofty vocation... and obligation to bring forth fruit in charity for the life of the world'.

Characterizing Virtue

While virtue itself may be said to be as old as the hills literature, both philosophical and theological, on the virtues

---

[340] See James D.G. Dunn, *The Theology of Paul the Apostle* (Edinburgh: T&T Clark, 1998), 662-665

[341] *The Ten Commandments and the Beatitudes* (New York: Rowan & Littlefield, A Sheed & Ward Book, 2012), 15

[342] See, for example, Daniel Harrington and James Keenan, *Jesus and Virtue Ethics – Building Bridges between New Testament Studies and Moral Theology* (New York: A Sheed & Ward Book, 2002)

has become a veritable growth industry.[343] Connecting virtue to character Tom Wright sees its transformation in terms of three steps – the identification of end/goal and means/steps and interiorization of 'those steps' so that they 'become habitual, a matter of second nature'.[344] If the habitual acquisition of a certain proficiency is said to demand ten thousand hours of practice, achieving excellence in the virtues could be a lifelong exercise. However, the Christian interpretation of virtue does not focus primarily on incessant individual effort aimed at achieving perfection on one's own but is founded on co-operation with the gift of grace which, in the words of Wright, is all about learning in advance the language of God's new world'.[345] The image of language indicates the communicative quality of virtue and the communal context in which goodness is both taught and learned.

In his survey of recent studies in biblical theology and theological ethics Lúcás Chan delineates the 'four dimensions of virtue ethics' which 'not only help us understand better the moral life but also make virtue a fuller ethical framework by serving as reference points to the task of hermeneutics'.[346] Firstly, the development of character in the course of a person's life demands a degree of integration of virtue as 'the ethics of virtue is

---

[343] For a helpful introduction see William C. Mattison III, *Introducing Moral Theology – True Happiness and the Virtues* (Grand Rapids, Michigan: Brazos Boos, 2008)

[344] *Virtue Reborn*, (London: SPCK, 2010), 27

[345] Ibid, 62

[346] *Biblical Ethics in The 21st Century* (New York: Paulist Press, 2013), 84-85 (see also his 'Notes on Moral Theology – Biblical Ethics: 3D', *Theological Studies*, 76 (2015):112-128)

all about moral formation'.[347] Secondly, this formation involves the development of habits which are acquired through practise. Aristotle's line about the just person acting justly illustrates the indexical relation between being and doing, performance and virtue. Thirdly, virtue ethics emphasizes the importance of moral exemplars in the development of character and display of habits that encourage others to imitate. Fourthly, criticism of virtue ethics as self-centred and subjective is countered by the logical contradiction contained in the concept of ethical privatization and by looking at the conception of the good as communal instead of individualistic. Thus, Jesus' vision of the Kingdom of God calls for the personal development and display of virtue by his disciples which draws others by their example into the community of the Church.

Luke as Virtue Ethicist

The evangelist indicates his interest in virtue from the beginning. Zechariah and Elizabeth are both described as being *dikaioi*, 'righteous before God', 'living blamelessly according to all the commandments and regulations of the Lord' (1:6).*The Jerusalem Bible* uses the same adjective in the angel alerting Zechariah that among the tasks of his son John is 'to turn... the disobedient back to the wisdom that the virtuous have, preparing for the Lord a people fit for him' (1:17). In turn, Zechariah himself proclaims that this state is one of 'serv[ing] him in holiness and virtue in his presence, all our days' (1:75). This is the call to be both holy and good, to combine worship

---

[347]   Ibid, 86

and works in the circumstances of everyday life and over the course of a lifetime. Prayer and praise of God are not apart from attitudes and actions towards others. This perception of integral and incarnational spirituality is of a piece with Luke's presentation of morality.

Described as 'righteous (*dikaios*) and devout' (2:25), Simeon personifies this spirit of holiness and virtue. A resident of Jerusalem and habitué of the Temple he is on hand 'when the parents brought in the child Jesus, to do for him what was customary under the law' (2:27). Picking up the child he praises God in a prayer of tender thanksgiving that has become immortalized in speech and song as the *Nunc dimittis*. Bovon comments that 'Jesus' reception by Simeon is a global behaviour and attitude, in which the entire person of the old man, his body and inner self, his thoughts and feelings, become active'.[348] As a summary of the stance of virtue this statement can hardly be surpassed. Simeon's willingness to depart the scene (and world) at the sight of the child Jesus asserts the fulfilment of the final words of the *Benedictus*. Announcing that he is able to be dismissed 'in peace, according to your word' (2:29), Simeon states that the expectation of Israel has been fulfilled. Moreover, in keeping with the evangelist's universalism, he expresses that his eyes 'have seen your salvation, which you have prepared in the presence of all peoples, a light for revelation to the Gentiles' (2:30-32). Through the birth and presentation of the Christ child all people are invited to 'serve [God] in holiness and virtue in his presence' all the days of their lives.

---

[348]   *Luke 1*, 101

Luke's version of the call of Levi carries a notable contrast with that of Matthew on two counts, one concerning an omission, the other involving an inclusion. In the course of Jesus' response to the complaint of the Pharisees to his disciples about his eating with tax-collectors and sinners, Matthew includes the proof text from Hosea, 'Go and learn what this means, 'I desire mercy, not sacrifice' (9:13). Brendan Byrne puts this prophetic prescription in context:

> The querulous Pharisees are not simply put right. They are given an interpretive task... Let them reflect upon the clear indication of divine will contained in the quotation and ponder its implications for applying the Torah to everyday life, including the social situation presently in view. They might then be less inclined to criticize Jesus and his disciples for celebrating with tax collectors and sinners the mercy and forgiveness of God. Jesus is "fulfilling" the Torah in the way Hosea 6:6 indicates to be what God wants, placing mercy before all other considerations.[349]

Luke's version of Jesus' response - 'Those who are well have no need of a physician, but those who are sick; I have come to call not the righteous but sinners to repentance' (5:31-32) – is the same as Matthew's without that evangelist's interpolation of the insistence of the priority of mercy. While the contrast is notable in the context of this study of mercy/compassion in Luke, it is not within its competence to comment on the question of the

---

[349] *Lifting the Burden - Reading Matthew's Gospel in the Church Today* (Collegeville, MN:Liturgical Press, 2004), 80-81

relationship of *Matthew* and *Luke* and their respective sources. Luke's addition to both Matthew and Mark of the call 'to repentance' emphasizes the evangelist's overall salvific intent and reiterates another major theme of his Gospel. Reflected in characters like Levi and Zacchaeus, repentance results in the righteousness that the virtuous realize in their relationships with God and others.

Bad press follows the Pharisees throughout *Luke*. After clashing with them on account of their love of money Jesus characterizes them as 'those who justify yourselves in the sight of others; but God knows your hearts; for what is prized by human beings is an abomination in the sight of God (16:15). To be considered unworthy in the sight of God is a severe cutback; to be castigated for their lack of virtue compounds the judgement. Their sense of righteousness is superficial and subject to social approval. As Patella states, 'In such a case, people will never do an act that may be good but unpopular'.[350] Two parables placed side by side show how the absence of virtue amounts to the adoption of attitudes of disdain and dismissal. The judge in the case of the widow who continually comes to him for redress is unjust because he 'neither feared God nor respected any human being' (18:2). Similarly the Pharisee personifies those 'who trusted in themselves that they were righteous and regarded others with contempt' (18:9). Luke concludes this latter parable by contrasting those who are humble with those who hold themselves in high esteem. Reference to the self-exalted recalls Mary's words in the *Magnificat* about the proud and powerful.

---

[350]   *The Gospel According To Luke*, 109

In contraposition the lowly will be lifted up and chief among these are the children whom Jesus calls to come to him because 'it is to such as these that the kingdom of God belongs' (18:17). Like the widow and the tax-collector in the preceding parables, the 'little children' are dependent and disposed to draw from the depths of God's compassion disclosed in Jesus.

Exemplarism is an essential element of virtue ethics. As Chan states, 'virtue ethics also appreciates the role that exemplary figures play in the development and formation of character'[351]. Presupposing that virtue can be learned (and therefore taught) this involves imitation and modelling of what it means to be(come) good through practice of certain character traits and types of conduct. There are many exemplary figures in *Luke* ranging from those in the early events involving the incarnation and infancy of Jesus through John the Baptist to Mary who was commended for having 'chosen the better part' (10:42). Women figure prominently among Luke's portrait of the virtuous. Barbara E. Reid sees Simon's mother-in-law as serving 'as a prototype of the disciple whose ministry of faithful attendance on another is modelled after the service that Jesus exemplified'.[352] The woman searching for the lost coin in the parable of the same name displays a sense of perseverance which Jesus proposes as a model for prayer. The strength of character shown by the widow in pursuit of justice stands in marked contrast to the judge who is described as being deficient in virtue. As an exemplar of enduring effort which eventually earns its due reward, the

---

[351] *The Ten Commandments and the Beatitudes* (Plymouth, UK: Rowman and Littlefield Publishers – A Sheed & Ward Book, 2012), 11
[352] *Choosing the Better Part?* 101

anonymous widow is a patron of all who advocate for justice, especially against opposition and obstruction.

For Luke the disciples are formed through following Jesus. They learn the way of discipleship through listening to his teaching and looking at the attitudes he portrays and the actions he performs. It is by travelling with him to Jerusalem that they gradually come to appreciate and accept the 'terms and conditions' of discipleship. Along the way the evangelist narrates encounters with people who exhibit a spectrum of virtue and vice extending from generosity, solidarity and mercy to greed, selfishness and mean spiritedness. Controversies with the Pharisees and other parties highlight the contrast between commitment to virtue or viciousness. The disciples – and readers – are left in no doubt as to which way Jesus calls them to follow. Noting that Luke 'loves the preposition *syn* = with', Anselm Grün admits it is through being 'with Jesus on the way' that 'he takes us with him on the way of transformation'.[353] This transformation is ultimately a destiny rather than a destination. Unlike John, Luke does not use images like light and life to symbolize this transformation but shows salvation as sharing in the mercy and forgiveness of God.

While Luke expresses that Jesus is the exemplar of virtue *par excellence* his main evangelical purpose is not to establish Jesus as a standard or model of goodness or even holiness. Luke's primary intent is 'indicative', in proclaiming Jesus as the Christ who enables people to experience the merciful love of

---

[353]   *Jesus: The Image of Humanity*, 81

God. As enabler the love that Jesus embodies as mercy is, in the succinct statement of Richard A. McCormick, 'primarily empowerment'.[354] The mercy of God manifest in Jesus is more than a model of morality as it means the reversal of a merit-based approach that esteems excellence as an end in itself and evaluates it in terms of earning it by one's own effort. God's 'great reversal' is the revelation of His mercy which allows people to receive and remain in the relationship Jesus offers with only one requirement, repentance that is open to receiving salvation. Thus the poor are lifted up from their lowly social status, the widow's son is raised to life and restored to her, the lepers recover their health and their rightful place in society, the wounded and abandoned are assisted to become well again, the profligate son finds a place in his father's house, the man who was poor during his life on earth enjoys eternal riches, the humble tax-collector can lift up his eyes to heaven in hope. By indicating God's mercy Jesus invites his followers to inhabit, imitate and incarnate it.

The Gospel Virtue

In their article aiming 'to give an account of Christian virtue ethics' Michael G. Lawler and Todd A. Salzman open with the statement that 'Jesus' parable of the Good Samaritan provides the key to what follows'.[355] Their approach advances 'virtue ethics as a normative ethics more promising to the moral life than

---

[354] *Health and Medicine in the Catholic Tradition* (New York: Crossroad, 1985), 37

[355] 'Virtue Ethics: Natural and Christian', *Theological Studies*, 74 (2013): 442-473, here 442

utilitarianism or deontology' which 'gives precedence not to the actions of the agents but to their personal characters formed in their respective moral communities and learned through the imitation of respected role models in those communities'.[356] This description raises two issues or objections that are often levelled against virtue ethics: it places too much emphasis on the character of the agent at the expense of the conduct of his/ her action; it ignores the communal dimension by concentrating on the individual. Lawler and Salzman address and answer the first criticism in the context of the parable: 'If we assume that the Good Samaritan acted with compassion and benevolence towards the injured man, he still could have chosen to act as did the two clerics, that is, without compassion or benevolence. In virtue ethics, virtuous acts, not merely the virtuous character state of the person doing the acts, are important'.[357] As they state elsewhere, 'if it is understood to mean that virtue ethics ignores *doing*, it is untrue, for we expect the virtuous person to *do* or *act* virtuously'.[358] William C. Spohn shows how the compassion of the Good Samaritan combines both vision and conduct:

> His compassion impels him to do something to help the victim. His subjective capacity of being receptive to suffering goes beyond pity to empathy; he "feels with" and "feels into" the situation by apprehending the situation as the man in the ditch experiences it. *Empathy* refers to the affective, imaginative, and cognitive capacity

---

[356] Ibid, 443

[357] Ibid, 461

[358] 'People Beginning Sexual Experience', in ed Adrian Thatcher, The Oxford Handbook of Theology, Sexuality, and Gender (Oxford: Oxford University Press, 2015), 557-571, here 562

that enables us to enter and identify with the experience of others. *Compassion* refers to the most active and engaged form of empathy, namely, that disposition directed particularly to those in great need or suffering. Compassion bridges the gap between perception and effective action.[359]

The second criticism of virtue ethics is countered by the fact that, for Luke, compassion is a core value for the community that Jesus created in the course of his ministry. Luke's communal focus of formation in following Jesus and furthering his mission is well formulated by Frank Matera: 'This community of disciples, at the centre of which are the twelve apostles, forms the nucleus of a repentant and restored Israel that will emerge as the Church in Acts, though its members will still be called disciples. The teaching which Jesus provides his disciples is the foundation for the moral life they will live in this community of like-minded disciples'.[360] Compassionate action by the community is directed towards care for the poor and sick and those who are marginalized or outcast, both socially and spiritually. For Luke compassion is a social virtue and this is shown through its concern and conduct for the common good.

While it has not traditionally been counted as one of the theological/moral virtues, Michael W. Austin, noted American claims that 'unlike many of the virtues... compassion is *in*'.[361]

---

[359] *Go and Do Likewise*, 90

[360] *New Testament Theology – Exploring Diversity and Unity* (Louisville: Westminster John Knox Press, 2007), 84

[361] 'Compassion', in eds Michael W. Austin and R. Douglas Geivett, *Being Good – Christian Virtues for Everyday Life* (Grand Rapids, Michigan: Eerdmans, 2012), 185-203, here 185

Commencing in the awareness of another's – often acute – pain or privation compassion creates a virtuous cycle of recognition, response and remedy where possible. This cycle of compassion contains cognitive and emotional elements that are complemented and completed in the conduct of a person (or group) to assist or alleviate the anxiety or agony of another (group). As Austin states, 'a commitment to and the embodiment of compassion involves belief, emotion, and action'.[362] Compassion – as the prefix *com* – connotes, always includes identification with the plight of another that initiates the intention to become involved on his or her behalf to make things better or at least bearable. Compassionate looking at the sadness and suffering of another leads to charitable caring for them, even at the cost to self. Gerard Mannion proclaims this poetically (with the assistance of a philosopher):

> Compassion is certainly a word that is richly evocative in so many ways but the Italians can go one better. As Schopenhauer remarked in the mid-nineteenth century, in Italian 'sympathy and pure love are expressed... by the same word, *pietà*'.[363]

For Luke the virtue of compassion plays the part John gives to love in his *Gospel* (and *Letters*). Both evangelists entwine the 'imperative' – 'go and do likewise' ('love one another') – with the 'indicative' – 'as your Father is merciful' ('as I have loved you'). Speaking of 'the deepest experiences of compassionate

---

[362] Ibid, 187
[363] 'Compassion as the Fundamental Basis of Morality', in eds Julie Clague, Bernard Hoose, Gerard Mannion, *Moral Theology for the Twenty-First Century* (Edinburgh: T&T Clark, 2008), 237-251, here 249

love, where divine mercy is known and received and then given'[364] Margaret A. Farley sees grace as the ground from which goodness grows towards the goal to be as generous as God. Faith in the Father's compassion is the foundation for the disciples to follow Jesus in the first place and secondly bear the fruit of compassion in their conduct and contact with others. Invitation to both imitation and incarnation inheres in the biblically based virtue ethics.

Partners in the Paschal Mercy

In a memorable phrase the Second Vatican Council called the Christian 'one who has been made a partner in the paschal mystery'.[365] Moreover, the Council proclaims 'that the Holy Spirit offers to all the possibility of being made partners, in a way known to God, in the paschal mystery'.[366] This possibility is premised on the promise that 'all are in fact called to one and the same destiny'.[367] While 'in a way known to God' obviously indicates the mystery of God's purpose it also offers an insight into the motivation of God. This motivation is made transparent by transposing 'partner[s] in the paschal mystery' to *partners in the paschal mercy*. It is by virtue of Jesus' life, death and resurrection in the power of the Holy Spirit that Luke proclaims what Sobrino calls 'the ultimacy of mercy'.[368] Luke unfolds this ultimacy in its universal outreach through the Church.

---

[364]   *Compassionate Respect* (New York: Paulist Press, 2002), 82
[365]   *Pastoral Constitution on the Church in the Modern World*, 22
[366]   Ibid
[367]   Ibid
[368]   *Where Is God?* (Maryknoll, New York: Orbis Books, 2004), 83

Luke's theological purpose is ultimately salvific, concerned with showing how, as Lucien Richard states, 'God reveals Godself in the history of Israel and in Jesus' ministry as a compassionate God' and that 'in Jesus it is revealed that compassion is more salvific than power'.[369] Throughout *Luke* the evangelist of salvation expresses the mystery of God's mercy made manifest in the sensibility and solidarity Jesus shows with suffering humanity in spite of its sinfulness. In *Remembering his Mercy*, Luke records that the mercy of God is the measure of salvation and Christ its mediator.

---

[369] *Christ the Self-Emptying of God* (New York: Paulist Press, 1997), 188

Postscript

Looking at Mercy and Luke
through a Papal Lens

In his homily at the *Missa Pro Eligendo Romano Pontifice* (Mass for the Election of the Roman Pontiff) in the Vatican Basilica on 12 March 2013 Cardinal Angelo Sodano begins with the opening line of Psalm 88(9) – 'Forever I will sing of the mercies of the Lord'. Taking up this theme he refers to the first reading from the prophet Isaiah: 'God announces that he will send a Messiah full of mercy, a Messiah who would say: "The spirit of the Lord God is upon me…he has sent me to bring good news to the poor, to bind up the wounds of broken hearts, to proclaim liberty to captives, freedom to prisoners, and to announce a year of mercy of the Lord" (Isaiah 61-1-3)'.[370] Speaking of the full realization of this prophecy in Jesus he says 'this mission of mercy has been entrusted to the pastors of his Church … but is especially entrusted to the Bishop of Rome, Shepherd of the universal Church'.[371] Coinciding with *Luke* – Year C in the Sunday Lectionary – Pope Francis has chosen to celebrate 'a year of mercy' in continuity with the papal mission of mercy.

---

[370] Homily of His Eminence Cardinal Angelo Sodano, Dean of the College of Cardinals (http://www.vatican.va/sede_vacante/3013/homily-pro-eligendo-pontifice_2013_en.html) [accessed 19/02/2015)

[371] Ibid

Opening the Second Vatican Council Pope Saint John XXIII uses the metaphors of medicine and maternity to manifest this mission of mercy. Referring to the Church as displaying 'the medicine of mercy rather than of severity' and desiring 'to show herself to be the loving mother of all... full of mercy'[372], Pope John's words resonate deeply with Luke's presentation of 'the Messiah full of mercy'. Maternity features heavily in the opening chapters of *Luke* in the figures of Elizabeth and Mary. Noting that 'in every story told about her Elizabeth displays a calm acceptance of God's movement of mercy towards her', Patricia A. Sharbaugh says that 'Elizabeth's realization of the depths of God's mercy is tied to [her] experience as mother'.[373] Relating how 'in Hebrew, the word mercy shares the same root as the word for womb (*rḥm*)' Sharbaugh states that 'metaphorically, motherhood is a condition that reveals to us the deeply rooted mercy of God'.[374] Offering her maternity to God in a paean of praise Mary literally prepares the way for Jesus and his Messianic mission which he announces in terms of the fulfilment of Isaiah's prophecy. Luke's expression of Jesus' longing 'to gather your children together as a hen gathers her brood under her wings' (13:34) is an image of 'brooding compassion'[375]

---

[372] Pope Saint John XXIII, 'Opening Address of the Second Vatican Council', 11 October 1962) in Jared Wicks, *Doing Theology* (New York: Paulist Press, 2009), 141-151, here 148

[373] 'Hannah, Elizabeth, and Mary: Models of Faithful waiting', *The Bible Today*, 50 (2012,165-169, here 169

[374] Ibid, 169

[375] This phrase is taken from the words of President Lyndon Johnson before the Lincoln Memorial on 12 February 1967 and quoted in Randall B. Woods, *LBJ – Architect of American Ambition* (New York: Free Press, 206), 786

which leads to his later tears over the City of Jerusalem. By linking maternity and medicine as the media for bearing and restoring life Luke lays the foundation for the Church's involvement in integral healthcare of people. However, given the original context of Pope John's words about mercy – 'the greatest concern of this Ecumenical Council is that the sacred deposit of Christian doctrine should be guarded and taught more efficaciously [as] that doctrine embraces the whole person'[376] – critical attention needs to be given to the caveat raised by Pope Francis in his call to the Association of Italian Catholic Doctors to resist 'the dominant thinking [that] sometimes suggests "a false compassion"'.[377]

Addressing the final session of the Second Vatican Council Pope Paul VI says that 'the parable of the Good Samaritan has been the model of the spirituality of the Council' and that 'a feeling of boundless sympathy has permeated the whole of it'.[378] This feeling is featured in the subsequent opening lines of the Council's final document – "The joys and hopes, the grief and anguish of the people of our time, especially of those who are poor or afflicted, are the joys and hopes, the grief and anguish of the followers of Christ as well'.[379] This sense of solidarity with humanity, especially with those who suffer,

---

[376]   Quoted in Wicks, *Doing Theology*, 146
[377]   'Pope urges doctors to witness to sanctity of life', (http://www.news.va/en/news/pope-urges-doctors-to-witness-to-sanctity-of-life),   [accessed 19/11/2014]
[378]   'Address at the Last Meeting of Vatican Council II', 7 December 1965, in Wicks, *Doing Theology*, 163-171, here 168
[379]   *Gaudium et Spes, Pastoral Constitution on the Church in the Modern World*, 1, in ed Flannery, *Vatican Council II, The Basic Sixteen Documents*

shows that the focus of the Council's 'rich teaching', in Paul VI's phrase, was 'channelled in one direction, the service of humankind, of every condition, in every weakness and need'.[380] Rejecting any flight from the world, this reiterates the Church's ongoing commitment to collaborate with all who fight injustice and inequalities across all indices in the world. By invoking the Parable of the Compassionate Samaritan as the spirituality permeating the Council Paul VI shows himself to be a Lucan Pope, inspired by the evangelist's message of help, healing and hope for the sick and poor, outcast and marginalized. Combining images of Jesus the *Man of Sorrows* and *Messiah of Mercy* Paul pleads 'how in everyone we can and must recognize the countenance of Christ, the Son of Man, especially when tears and sorrows make it plain to see, and if we can and must recognize in Christ's countenance the countenance of our heavenly Father'.[381] This conciliar spirituality is well captured by Paul's successor, Pope John Paul I who, earlier in 1965 when, as Cardinal Albino Luciani, began a series of talks to priests from the Veneto region in his inimitable style: 'The Good Samaritan is Jesus, the unlucky wayfarer is we ourselves. He recognized human frailty, of our need to help ourselves and each other, with God's help, telling a charming little parable of his own to illustrate his point'.[382]

In his encyclical *Dives in misericordia (Rich in mercy)* Pope John Paul II states the need to delve into the teaching of the

---

[380] 'Address at the Last Meeting of Vatican Council II', in Wicks, *Doing Theology*, 169

[381] Ibid, 170-171

[382] Quoted in Paul Spackman, *God's Candidate – The Life and Times of Pope John Paul I* (Leominster, Herefordshire: Gracewing, 2008), 55

Second Vatican Council about the paschal mystery of Christ's death and resurrection 'if we wish to express in depth the truth about mercy'.[383] In a moving paragraph he speaks about how, in the course of his passion, Jesus 'himself seems to merit the greatest mercy', 'to appeal for mercy' and 'deserves mercy from the people to whom he has done good'.[384] This is very close to Luke's portrayal of Jesus, particularly in his agony in Gethsemane where the evangelist expresses how 'in his anguish he prayed more earnestly, and his sweat became like great drops of blood falling down to the ground' (22:44). In his suffering John Paul II states that Jesus 'addresses himself to the Father – that Father whose love he has preached to people, to whose mercy he has borne witness through all of his activity'.[385] John Paul II goes on to link love and mercy, 'for mercy is an indispensable dimension of love; it is as it were love's second name'.[386] In a moving sentence he states that 'in human history, which is at the same time the history of sin and death, love must be revealed above all as mercy and must also be actualized as mercy'.[387] This emphasis on the revelation and realization of mercy is related to his own dedication to the writings of Saint Faustina Kowalska and devotion to the Divine Mercy.

Divine Mercy is distilled in a number of declarations of Pope Benedict XVI. Reflecting on the *Parable of the Compassionate Parent/Prodigal Son* in Lent 2010 he proclaimed:

---

[383] *Dives in misericordia*, 7
[384] Ibid
[385] Ibid
[386] Ibid
[387] Ibid, 8

This passage of Saint Luke constitutes one of the peaks of spirituality and literature of all time. Indeed, what would our culture, art and more generally our civilization be without this revelation of a God, the Father so full of mercy? It never fails to move us and every time we hear or read it, it can suggest to us ever new meanings. Above all, this Gospel text has the power of speaking to us of God, of enabling us to know his face and better still, His Heart.[388]

Under the heading – *God the merciful Father will never cease seeking us in love* – Benedict brings out his predecessor's words about how 'love must be revealed above all as mercy and must also be actualized as mercy'. If this biblical text can ever engender new meanings, the mission of divine mercy can never be exhausted for God is 'so full of mercy'. This recalls Luke's line in the parable about the father who 'was filled with compassion' (15:20). The revelation and realization of God's mercy historically and universally – two of Luke's major themes are touched on in Benedict's words about 'contemplating the merciful God's action in history, feeling tangibly the saving effects of the Cross and of the Resurrection of Christ, in every epoch and for every person'.[389] The Marian dimension of mercy is highlighted in 'With a mother's tenderness, she wants to make us understand that our whole life should be a response to the love of our God, who is so rich in

---

[388] *L'Osservatore Romano*, Weekly English edition, 17 March 2010, 1
[389] 'The last word on evil is the mercy of God', *L'Osservatore Romano*, Weekly English edition, 30 March 2011, 5

mercy'.[390] For Benedict 'the consolation of God's compassionate love' means that 'the star of hope rises'.[391]

'Horizon' and 'mercy' are two main themes that figure prominently in the teaching of Pope Francis. Horizon is more than geography, though he often uses spatial images as in his call to go to the 'peripheries'. For him horizon is both the herald and hope for the Gospel while the Gospel is the Good News of God's mercy. Together these words form the key hermeneutic of his message and mission: 'horizon of mercy'. From the outset of his papal mission he has operated within this.[392] In an address to the aptly named Italian *Misericordie* he states the core of Christian compassion:

> "*Misericordia*" [mercy], a Latin word whose etymological meaning is "*miseris cor dare*", to "give the heart to the wretched", those in need, those who are suffering. That is what Jesus did: he opened his heart to the wretchedness of man. The Gospel has a wealth of episodes which present the *misericordia* of Jesus, his love freely given for the suffering and the weak. From the Gospel narratives we are able to understand the closeness, the goodness, the tenderness with which Jesus drew in the suffering

---

[390] 'Life as a response to God's love', *L'Osservatore Romano*, Weekly English edition, 28 September 2011, 13

[391] *Spe Salvi* (Encylical Letter on Christian Hope), (London: Catholic Truth Society, 2007), 39.k

[392] See Walter Kasper, 'Mercy – The Key Word of his Pontificate', Chapter V, *Pope Francis' Revolution of Tenderness and Love* (New York: Paulist Press, 2015), 31-36

people and consoled them, comforted them, and often healed them. By our Teacher's example, we too are called to draw near, to share the conditions of the people we meet.[393]

In *Evangelii Gaudium/The Joy of the Gospel* Francis proposes mercy as 'the greatest of all the virtues' and proclaims that 'the Church must be a place of mercy freely given, where everyone can feel welcomed, loved, forgiven and encouraged to live the good life of the Gospel'.[394] Francis combines both the virtue of mercy and the Church as its vehicle in his vision for the forthcoming *Extraordinary Jubilee of Mercy*. Coinciding with the *Year of Luke* there is ample material for reflection on the meaning of mercy as both motive and material for the mission of the Church.[395] From healthcare to helping the broken-hearted, reaching out to those on the margins (Francis' 'peripheries') and reconciling sinners, the Gospel of Luke gives examples and encouragement for envisaging evangelization as the expression and enactment of God's mercy in Christ through the Holy

---

[393] 'Address of Pope Francis to the National Confederation of the "*Misericordie*" of Italy on the occasion of the anniversary of its meeting with Pope John Paul II on 14 June 1986' (http://w2.vatican.va/content/francesco/en/speeches/2014/june/documents/papa-frances) [accessed 03/03/2015]

[394] For a commentary see Paolo Benanti, TOR, 'La gioia del Vangelo nel cambio anthropologico', *Gregorianum,* 96(2015), 77-97, especially 86-96, 'Dal cuore del Vangelo: La misericordia come risposta' ('From the heart of the Gospel: Mercy as Response'), (My translation)

[395] In his reflections for the Argentinian National Day at the Metropolitan Cathedral in Buenos Aires Cardinal Bergoglio chose texts from *Luke* for five of the years between 1999 and 2004. For details see Mario I. Aguilar, *Pope Francis – His Life and Thought* (Cambridge, U.K.: The Lutterworth Press, 2014), 136

Spirit. It is fitting to finish with the final words of Francis at the Yad Vashem Memorial in Jerusalem: 'Remember us in your mercy'.[396]

---

[396] 'Visit to the Yad Vashem Memorial – Pilgrimage to the Holy Land on the Occasion of the 50th Anniversary of the meeting between Pope Paul VI and Patriarch Athenagoras in Jerusalem, http://w2.vatican.va/content/francesco/en/speeches/2014/may/documents/papa-frances)   [accessed 03/03/2015]

Select Bibliography

Jean-Noël Aletti, *Le Jésus De Luc*, Paris: MamE-Desclée, 2010

Elena Bosetti, *Luke – The Song of God's Mercy*, Boston: Pauline, 2006

François Bovon, *Luke the Theologian*, Waco, Texas: Baylor University Press, (2nd Revised edition), 2006

_____. *Luke 1* (A Commentary on the Gospel of Luke 1:1-9:50), Minneapolis: Fortress Press, 2002

_____. *Luke 2*, (A Commentary on the Gospel of Luke 9:51-19:27), Minneapolis: Fortress Press, 2013

John R. Donahue, *The Gospel in Parable*, Fortress Press, 1988C.F. Evans, *Saint Luke*, London: SCM Press, 1990

Joseph A. Fitzmyer, *The Gospel According to Luke (X-XXIV)*, New York: Doubleday & Company, 1985

Luke Timothy Johnson, *The Gospel of Luke*, Collegeville, MN: The Liturgical Press, 1991

Robert J. Karris, *Luke: Artist and Theologian*, New York: Paulist Press, 1985

Michael Mullins, *The Gospel of Luke*, Dublin: The Columba Press, 2010

Mikeal C. Parsons, *Luke – Storyteller, Interpreter, Evangelist,* Peabody, Mass: Hendrickson Publishers, 2007

Michael F. Patella, *The Gospel According to Luke,* Collegeville, MN: Liturgical Press, 2005

Pope Benedict XVI/Joseph Ratzinger, *Jesus of Nazareth,* London: Bloomsbury, 2007

Barbara E. Reid, *Choosing the Better Part? – Women in the Gospel of Luke,* Collegevile, MN: The Liturgical Press, 1996

Barbara Shellard, *New Light on Luke – Its Purpose, Sources and Literary Content,* London: Sheffield Academic Press, 2002

Klyne R. Snodgrass, *Stories with Intent – A Comprehensive Guide to the Parables of Jesus,* Cambridge, U.K.: Eerdmans, 2008

Robert C. Tannehill, *The Narrative Unity of Luke-Acts: A Literary Interpretation, Volume 1: The Gospel according to Luke,* Philadelphia: Fortress Press, 1986